The revelation God gave to Bill Bright that literally charged his life with divine power was the Person, purpose, presence, and power of the Holy Spirit, and His vital relevance to every believer's life.

From the Foreword by
KAY ARTHUR

BILL BRIGHT'S
"THE JOY OF KNOWING GOD"
SERIES

SPIRIT-FILLED
LIVING

DR. BILL BRIGHT

Victor®

The Bible Teacher's Teacher

COOK COMMUNICATIONS MINISTRIES
Colorado Springs, Colorado • Paris, Ontario
KINGSWAY COMMUNICATIONS LTD
Eastbourne, England

Victor® is an imprint of
Cook Communications Ministries,
Colorado Springs, CO 80918
Cook Communications, Paris, Ontario
Kingsway Communications, Eastbourne, England

THE JOY OF SPIRIT-FILLED LIVING
© 2005 by Bill Bright

First Printing, 2005
Printed in the United States of America
1 2 3 4 5 6 7 8 9 10 Printing/Year 09 08 07 06 05

Cover Design: Brand Navigation, LLC

Library of Congress Cataloging-in-Publication Data

Bright, Bill.
    The joy of spirit-filled living : the power to succeed / Bill Bright.
        p. cm. -- (The joy of knowing God ; Bk. 3)
    ISBN 0-7814-4248-6 (pbk.)
    1. Success--Religious aspects--Christianity. 2. Holy Spirit. I. Title.
    BV4598.25.B75 2005
                        231'.3--dc22
                                            2004026881

Dedication

GLOBAL FOUNDING PARTNERS

The Bright Media Foundation continues the multifaceted ministries of Bill and Vonette Bright for generations yet unborn. God has touched and inspired the Brights through the ministries of writers through the centuries. Likewise, they wish to pass along God's message in Jesus Christ as they have experienced it, seeking to inspire, train, and transform lives, thereby helping to fulfill the Great Commission each year until our Lord returns.

*Many generous friends have prayed and sacrificed to support the Bright Media Foundation's culturally relevant, creative works, in print and electronic forms. The following persons specifically have helped to establish the foundation. These spe*cial friends will always be known as Global Founding Partners *of the Bright Media Foundation.*

Bill and Christie Heavener and family

Stuart and Debra Sue Irby and family

Edward E. Haddock Jr., Edye Murphy-Haddock, and the Haddock family

Acknowledgments

It was my privilege to share fifty-four years, six months, and twenty days of married life with a man who loved Jesus passionately and served Him faithfully. Six months before his home going, Bill initiated what has become "The Joy of Knowing God" series. It was his desire to pass along to future generations the insights God had given him that they, too, could discover God's magnificence and live out the wonderful plan He has for their lives.

"The Joy of Knowing God" series is a collection of Bill Bright's top ten life-changing messages. Millions of people around the world have already benefited greatly from these spiritual truths and are now living the exciting Christian adventure that God desires for each of us.

On behalf of Bill, I want to thank the following team that helped research, compile, edit, and wordsmith the manuscripts and audio scripts in this series: Jim Bramlett, Rebecca Cotton, Eric Metaxas, Sheryl Moon, Cecil Price, Michael Richardson, Eric Stanford, and Rob Suggs.

I also want to thank Bill's longtime friends and Campus Crusade associates Bailey Marks and Ted Martin, who carefully reviewed the scripts and manuscripts for accuracy.

Bill was deeply grateful to Bob Angelotti and Don Stillman of Allegiant Marketing Group for their encouragement to produce this series and their ingenuity in facilitating distribution to so many.

A special thanks to Cook Communications and its team of dedicated professionals who partnered with Bright Media Foundation in this venture, as well as to Steve Laube, who brought us together.

Last but not least, I want to express my appreciation to Helmut Teichert, who worked faithfully and diligently in overseeing this team that Bill's vision would be realized, and to John Nill, CEO of Bright Media, who has helped me navigate the many challenges along this journey.

As a result of the hard work of so many, and especially our wonderful Lord's promise of His grace, I trust that multitudes worldwide will experience a greater joy by knowing God and His ways more fully.

With a grateful heart,
MRS. BILL BRIGHT (VONETTE)

Contents

Foreword

Early in his life, Bill Bright discovered a great truth—a truth neglected by many as their focus turned to the wisdom, ability, and power of man. Bill spent the rest of his life telling people about this truth, being used of God to transform lives all over the world.

The Lord, through his prophet Zechariah, proclaimed this truth millenniums ago: "'Not by might nor by power, but by My Spirit,' says the LORD of hosts" (Zechariah 4:6 NASB). Of course, the term Holy Spirit has been a part of church liturgy for almost two thousand years, but to many it was only a term, a confession repeated in the Apostles creed, rather than a Person, one of the Triune Godhead.

The revelation God gave to Bill Bright that literally charged his life with divine power was the Person, purpose, presence, and power of the Holy Spirit, and His vital relevance to every believer's life.

The truth about a life lived in the power of the Holy Spirit had been virtually buried in the religious traditions of mainstream believers. God used Bill Bright to resurrect it!

Understanding God's command to "be filled with the Spirit" (Ephesians 5:18 NASB), Bill's passion became "The Spirit-Filled Life." He wanted people to know what it meant to be filled with the Spirit, why it was so important, and how a person can be obedient to that command and consistently walk in that spiritual dimension. You will discover this inspiring message in the pages of this book.

Those five small words—"be filled with the Spirit"—really

became the linchpin of the vast worldwide movement of Campus Crusade for Christ International. Tens of thousands of full-time and part-time staff have carried this message and the gospel to virtually every country and in every major language. Literally billions all over the globe have heard the message of God's great love and forgiveness, and tens of millions have indicated their decision to trust Christ.

It is our prayer that as you read Bill's legacy, you will go to the Bible inductively, see what God says for yourself, and then walk according to faith's obedience. This was—I should say *is*—Bill's heart.

—KAY ARTHUR

1

Longing for Intimacy

Have you ever hit rock bottom and wondered how you had gotten there?

Just when we find ourselves moving along under the illusion that we are self-sufficient, handling life well, and standing on our own two feet, life has a way of reminding us that we are but small, helpless children. We discover there are forces too great for us to overcome alone. So we run crying to God, seeking comfort and answers.

But how does this square with Jesus' promise: "I tell you the truth, anyone who has faith in me will do what I have been doing. He will do even greater things than these, because I am going to the Father. And I will do whatever you ask in my name, so that the Son may bring glory to the Father. You may ask me for anything in my name, and I will do it" (John 14:12–14 NIV)?

Many years ago I was struck with this question: If Jesus' promise is true, then why do we struggle so much? How can God be with us and within us, yet so many of us live as though we're barely aware of His presence? I am convinced that it is because we tend to face life's problems without taking advantage of His wisdom. We cope with crises without calling upon the limitless strength that He has to offer us.

Why do we allow this to happen?

———————❖———————

How sincere are you in calling upon the Lord?

It certainly is not because God wants it to be so. Psalm 145:18 assures us, "The LORD is close to all who call on him, yes, to all who call on him sincerely." That means the Lord longs to maintain an intimate relationship with every one of us.

I believe the key word in that promise is *sincerely*. How sincere are you in calling upon the Lord? Do you really want to have a daily dependence upon Him? Or are you simply looking for instant help for the immediate problem of the moment? Do you wish to partake in a rich and full relationship with the King of Kings? Or are you concerned that He might interfere with the way you want to run your life?

Impure motives will never cause God to stop reaching out to you, but they will make it much more difficult for you to know the fullness of His love and power. Only when we finally come to a sincere desire for Him will we discover what He has wanted us to have all along.

THE HOLY SPIRIT AND YOU

The moment you accept God's gift of salvation and receive Christ into your life, He enters your heart in the Person of the Holy Spirit. Though you may not always be aware of Him, the Spirit takes permanent residence inside you. If you are a Christian, the Spirit of Christ remains within you every moment of every day. He is part of your life, available to empower and guide you whenever you sincerely call on Him.

Have you ever stopped to ponder how the Holy Spirit ministers to your life? Here are just some of the many blessings He bestows on those who trust in Him:

- He transforms our lives through a new birth.
- He provides comfort to us in difficult times.
- He strengthens us when we are weak.
- He intercedes for us even when we do not know how to pray.
- He teaches us God's truth.
- He bears witness with our spirit that we belong to God.
- He sets us apart for holy service to the Lord.
- He refreshes us deep in our souls.
- He produces the fruit of the Spirit in our lives.
- He unifies all believers everywhere.
- He enables us to lead holy lives that are pleasing to God.
- He brings us the ultimate joy and gives us a deep, inner peace that nothing can disturb.
- Above all, He empowers us to complete the mission Jesus Christ came to accomplish—to seek and save the lost.

You can experience the joy of Spirit-filled living—today and every day! Join me for an inspiring journey as we explore who the Holy Spirit is, how He gives you the power to succeed in your Christian walk, and how you can be filled with that power every moment of every day.

WE HAVE NO POWER WITHIN OURSELVES TO
SERVE GOD; SUPERNATURAL POWER IS NEEDED,
AND THE HOLY SPIRIT PROVIDES IT.

Who Is the Holy Spirit?

W hen you discover what it means for the Holy Spirit to be active in your life, you experience a power greater than anything on earth. But the modern world's ignorance of the Holy Spirit is far more pervasive than most of us realize.

Not long ago Christian pollster George Barna surveyed the beliefs of a Bible-believing church in California. It sounds unbelievable, but more than half of the congregation did not believe that the Holy Spirit is a living entity.

It seems some basic teaching is in order. Let us take a look at three basic attributes of the Holy Spirit.

THE HOLY SPIRIT IS NOT AN "IT"

T he Scriptures tell us that the Holy Spirit is a Person, just as Jesus is a Person and God the Father is a Person. Many people think of the Holy Spirit as some kind of will or force within them—not a *He* but an *it*. They confuse Him with the vague generic idea of a conscience or pick up false ideas from Eastern religions about some small "spark" of God within mankind. But the Bible is very clear that none of these views accurately describes who the Holy Spirit is and how He relates to us.

God's Spirit is fully a Person with all His own individual traits. He speaks, inspires, guides, convicts, comforts, and encourages—all functions an individual personality might perform. Jesus always referred to Him in that light, using the personal pronouns *He* and *Him*. When He spoke to the disciples in the Upper Room about the Holy Spirit, He used the Greek word *paracletos*, meaning "called to one's side." That name tells us that the Holy Spirit has the ability to give aid and to comfort or console.

God's Spirit is a Person with a vibrant and powerful personality. He is a unique member of the Trinity. As you learn more about His work in your life, you

---❖---

The Holy Spirit possesses all the attributes of God.

---

will be more aware of His presence and power. You will recognize His gentle voice, welcome His comfort, and bask in His encouragement. He will become a perfect friend who is with you everywhere you go.

THE HOLY SPIRIT IS GOD

The Bible proclaims that God is one, yet triune. That is, He exists as three Persons in one. How can God be one and three at the same time? The Bible has many references to the fact that God is triune. At creation, God declared, "Let *us* make people in our image, to be like ourselves" (Genesis 1:26). After mankind fell into sin, the Lord God said, "The people have become as *we* are, knowing everything, both good and evil" (Genesis 3:22). Romans 1:4 says, "Jesus Christ our Lord was shown to be the Son of God when God powerfully raised him from the dead by means of the Holy Spirit."

The Holy Spirit is coequal with God the Father and God the Son (John 14:16). He possesses all the attributes of God. The Scriptures tell us that the Holy Spirit is:

> all-powerful,
> all-knowing,
> ever-present,
> sovereign,
> holy,
> absolute truth,
> righteous,
> just,
> loving,
> merciful,
> faithful, and
> never-changing.

He is not a servant of God or a lesser expression of God. He is in every sense the living God.

THE SPIRIT'S MISSION

The Holy Spirit has a specific mission in our lives. He has been at work in the world since creation, and He temporarily indwelt certain individuals in the Old Testament for specific purposes. When He came at Pentecost, however, it was to permanently indwell all believers and to accomplish a network of missions and ministries.

The Spirit convicts the world of sin and leads us into all truth. It is through the Holy Spirit's work in our lives that we come to recognize our sin and our need for a Savior. He then draws us to God's truth and to the salvation that is available only through Jesus Christ.

The Holy Spirit glorifies Jesus. This is one of the primary ways we recognize the Spirit in someone's life: If Jesus is exalted and held high, this is a sign that the Holy Spirit is at work. Believers who are controlled by the Spirit will not take the credit for the good things they accomplish in His power; the glory is always directed toward Jesus Christ.

Do you long to live a more consistent Christian life?

Another mission of the Holy Spirit is to empower believers. Just before Jesus was crucified, He made the most startling promise of His entire ministry to His disciples. He proclaimed, "The truth is, anyone who believes in me will do the same works I have done, and even greater works, because I am going to be with the Father. You can ask for anything in my name, and I will do it" (John 14:12–13). The disciples must have been stunned! Jesus fed thousands and enabled the blind to see. The truth is that we have no power within ourselves to serve God; supernatural power is needed, and the Holy Spirit provides it.

The disciples were powerless even with the constant presence of Jesus among them. But after the Holy Spirit came at Pentecost, they boldly proclaimed the good news of Jesus' resurrection. The entrance of the Spirit into the lives of the first Christians was like turning on a power transformer.

YOUR KEY TO ABUNDANT LIVING

Do you long to live a more consistent Christian life? Is the Holy Spirit filling you daily and equipping you for service, or do you feel the frustration of trying to live the supernatural life by natural means?

Do you long to overcome past failures and destructive habits and experience a victorious life?

Do you long for your marriage, your relationships, and your work to move beyond the commonplace and reflect the amazing love and integrity of Christ?

Have you been frustrated or fearful about sharing your faith? Do you wish for your life to further God's marvelous eternal plan?

Then you must surrender yourself to God's presence within you—His Holy Spirit!

God wants you to experience a life of excitement and fulfillment. Jesus came, and then sent His Spirit, so that you could "have life, and have it abundantly" (John 10:10 NASB). That life is available only when you experience the enabling of the Holy Spirit as a way of life. He will draw you every day to know Him in a deeper, more intimate way.

———————❖———————

"You shall receive power when the Holy Spirit has come upon you; and you shall be My witnesses both in Jerusalem, and in all Judea and Samaria, and even to the remotest part of the earth."

—Jesus Christ

——————————————

3

"You Shall Receive Power ..."

Have you ever thought how much easier it would be to live the Christian life if only you had lived when Jesus lived?

"If only I could talk to Jesus as the disciples were able to do!" we say. "If only I could sit at His feet, hear His teachings, and see His miracles. Life would be so much simpler and so much less frightening if I had God in the flesh right here beside me. I would never be tempted the way I am tempted right now and I wouldn't have fallen into sin the way I have."

Yes, it would be wonderful to look into the eyes of Jesus and ask Him the deepest questions of our lives. But have you ever studied the disciples' lives before and after the Holy Spirit came to them? The difference could not be more dramatic.

The four Gospels present the disciples as being rather childish and inept when Jesus was among them physically. They were often slow to understand the concepts He taught. They held many of the same misconceptions and prejudices as the general population of that time. They had rivalries and quarrels that are almost embarrassing for us to read about today. Anyone might have wondered how these disciples could ever be capable of carrying on the ministry that Jesus began.

❖

Jesus' arrest left the disciples frightened, discouraged, and defeated.

When He led His inner circle of disciples to pray with Him in the garden, they kept falling asleep. Then when He was arrested, their courage failed. All except John fled in terror and fear, despite all the wonderful things they had seen Him do. After His crucifixion, they made no attempt even to claim His body or help with funeral arrangements.

FROM BASHFUL TO BOLD

The disciples were Jesus' best and closest friends, but His arrest left them frightened, discouraged, and defeated. If the story had ended there, it is likely no gospels would ever have been written—and Jesus would be an obscure footnote in Jewish history. Praise God that the greatest story ever told did not end there!

When Jesus left them for the final time He promised, "You shall receive power when the Holy Spirit has come upon you; and you shall be My witnesses both in Jerusalem, and in all Judea and Samaria, and even to the remotest part of the earth" (Acts 1:8 NASB). And on the day of Pentecost He sent the Holy Spirit to fill them with courage and power. History is quite clear about the quality of the disciples' lives after that event!

They were indeed completely different, due to the transformation the Holy Spirit brought about in their hearts. Despite the intimidating power of the massive Roman Empire and the religious leaders who refused to acknowledge Jesus as

Messiah, these same disciples became bold, tireless men who changed the history of the world.

The Spirit of God brings the most amazing power that can possibly be released upon the world. It was true in the days of the early Christian church, and it is still true today. God wants you to walk in the same power and victory as those world-shaking disciples of two thousand years ago.

"I have been crucified with Christ and I
no longer live, but Christ lives in me.
The life I live in the body, I live by faith in
the Son of God, who loved me
and gave himself for me."

Galatians 2:20 niv

4

The Holy Spirit and You

If you have sincerely asked Jesus to come into your life as your Savior, Lord, and Master, then the Holy Spirit has already made a home in your heart. The moment you surrendered your life to Jesus, the Spirit came in—even if you did not feel anything. Our faith is not based on feelings, it is based on facts.

Over the years I have used a simple diagram of a train to help illustrate the role of feelings and facts in our salvation and Spirit-led walk. The train is pulled by FACT, which is fueled by the FAITH car. FEELING is the caboose. We are to be fact-driven, not feeling-driven believers. (Since more people now use airlines than trains, I also employ the metaphor of an airliner to convey the same principle, as you'll see in appendix A.)

After the Spirit comes into your life through the new birth, He remains in residence. Why, then, do so many believers see no evidence of that fact? Why do they feel powerless?

WHAT'S HOLDING YOU BACK?

The answer is that it is one thing to *host* the Holy Spirit, and it is another to be *filled with* (guided, empowered, and controlled by) the Holy Spirit. It has often been said that the Spirit can be *resident* without being *"president."* You can yield control to Him all of the time, some of the time, or none of the time.

❖

Next to salvation itself, this is perhaps the greatest spiritual decision you can make.

Next to salvation itself, this is perhaps the greatest spiritual decision you can make.

It is up to you, every moment of every day. You have the free will to either obey God or disobey Him.

What, then, are the main obstacles that prevent Christians from being filled with the Holy Spirit?

PRIDEFUL SELF-RELIANCE

The first obstacle is *prideful self-reliance.* Pride is the most basic of sins; it confronts each of us. Our pride places our own will on the throne of our lives, rather than Christ. This "me-first" attitude, of course, is totally contrary to the Scriptures.

God's Word reminds me that I am crucified, dead, buried, and raised to newness of life with Christ (Romans 6). My flesh, the old Bill Bright, is at war with God. It never did please God and never will (Romans 8:7). It wars against Him!

So I must daily acknowledge that the old Bill Bright is dead. I, the new Bill Bright, am alive to Christ, and I freely and joyfully invite Him, in all of His resurrection love and power, to control my thoughts, desires, attitudes, actions, and words.

As the apostle Paul states in Galatians 2:20, "I have been crucified with Christ and I no longer live, but Christ lives in me. The life I live in the body, I live by faith in the Son of God, who loved me and gave himself for me" (NIV).

WORLDLINESS

The second obstacle is what Christians call *worldliness*. God made a glorious world, but because of our sinful nature we often become seduced by the treasures of this world and make idols of them; we lose sight of the One who created them in the first

"How do you benefit if you gain the whole world but lose your own soul?"
—Jesus Christ

place! Jesus proclaimed to His followers, "How do you benefit if you gain the whole world but lose your own soul in the process?" (Mark 8:36). In 1 Corinthians 7:31 we are told that "this world and all it contains will pass away."

Many years ago, Vonette and I made a commitment in writing—a commitment that we would not fall prey to worldliness but instead sign over every present and future material, intellectual, and spiritual possession to Him. That covenant has been the very key to any success we have enjoyed in ministry and in helping to build God's kingdom.

DESIRE FOR OTHERS' APPROVAL

The third obstacle to a Spirit-filled life is *undue desire for the approval of others*. Worrying too much about popular opinion can utterly destroy all that God would like to do in your life. Next to Jesus Christ, King Solomon was the wisest man who ever lived. He wrote, "The fear of man brings a snare, but he who trusts in the LORD will be exalted" (Proverbs 29:25 NASB). Each of us must be certain we are hearing directly from God, who alone knows what He has planned for us. And we must not let friends, even well-meaning Christian friends, confuse God's purpose and plans for our lives.

LACK OF FAITH

Another obstacle to Spirit-powered living is a simple *lack of faith.* Some believers cannot summon the will to place themselves completely in God's hands. That is why we must become clear about what Scripture says. The Bible tells us that God knew us even before He formed us in the womb. He cherishes the plans He has for us, as any father does for his child; Scripture tells us unequivocally that He loves us more than we can ever imagine. We must get that straight so we can trust Him totally, really trust Him—otherwise everything else will be a pale shadow of what He has planned for us. Have you truly trusted Christ not just as your Savior, but also as your Lord, Master, and King?

For more than fifty years, my wife and I have made every effort to take God at His Word, by faith, and we can assure you that He is more than faithful. As I mentioned, as a couple we signed away our lives to God one Sunday afternoon over half a century ago. We have never looked back. We literally wrote out and signed a contract, committing ourselves to live as bond servants of Jesus.

Approximately twenty-four hours after signing that contract, God gave me the vision for a worldwide movement to help fulfill the Great Commission, a movement we named Campus Crusade for Christ. I sincerely believe that had we not signed that contract, God would not have given me that vision.

No doubt, the millions who have been drawn to Christ through the Campus Crusade ministry are the direct fruit of that faithful leap into our Father's arms in which we trusted Him completely. Thousands of our fellow staff later joined us in total surrender to Him.

Unconfessed Sin

A fifth obstacle to the Spirit-filled life is *unconfessed sin.* Although Jesus has provided forgiveness for all sins—past, present, and future—we can still rob ourselves of intimacy with God through our disobedience. The prophet Isaiah offers us a perfect description of this regular event in the lives of all believers: "There is a problem—your sins have cut you off from God. Because of your sin, he has turned away and will not listen anymore" (Isaiah 59:2).

In order to stay in intimate fellowship with our loving Lord, we must confess any sin of thought, word, or deed as soon as we become aware of it. James 4:8 admonishes, "Draw close to God, and God will draw close to you. Wash your hands, you sinners; purify your hearts, you hypocrites."

> *To confess sin is to agree with God that we have stepped away from His path.*

To confess sin is to agree with God that we have stepped away from His path and to repent of our rebellion against Him. Honest confession with a truly repentant heart enables us to experience God's wonderful cleansing: "If we confess our sins, He is faithful and righteous to forgive us our sins and to cleanse us from all unrighteousness" (1 John 1:9 NASB). When we confess our sins, our relationship with the holy God is restored to newness and greater intimacy.

It is the Holy Spirit who points out unconfessed sin in our lives so that we can keep "short accounts" with our loving heavenly Father. I hope you make a habit of immediately confessing your sins as they occur. This practice is key to staying empowered and controlled by the Holy Spirit, and to experiencing the abundant life Christ promised.

5

How to Be Filled with the Spirit

Now that we've taken a quick look at who the Holy Spirit is and the common impediments that can prevent us from experiencing His daily power and guidance, the question remains: How can you and I experience the wonderful filling (moment-by-moment guidance, empowerment, and control) of the Holy Spirit?

In this chapter we will see from the Scriptures how we can do just that.

ACKNOWLEDGE YOUR THIRST

Because our wonderful God does not force Himself upon anyone, we must sincerely desire to be filled with His Spirit. Do you long to stop trying to live the successful Christian life on your own efforts and be empowered and controlled by Him? Listen to the invitation of Jesus:

> Jesus stood and shouted to the crowds, "If you are thirsty, come to me! If you believe in me, come and drink! For the Scriptures declare that rivers of living water will flow out

from within." (When he said "living water," he was speaking of the Spirit, who would be given to everyone believing
in him. But the Spirit had not yet been given, because
Jesus had not yet entered into his glory.)

JOHN 7:37-39

Are you thirsty to know Jesus in a deeper, more meaningful way? Are you thirsty to have a relationship with the Lord
that is more intimate than you ever thought possible? Then
come to the Lord and drink. Drink deeply of His Holy Spirit
and know life more abundant and fulfilling than you have ever
known before.

You need only ask Him. He is overjoyed when His children
come with this request, and He will be quick to fill you with
His Spirit.

CLEAR THE SLATE

Second, we must confess all disobedience to God. Sin short-
circuits our fellowship with God. It pollutes our prayers and
deadens our ability to hear His voice. Confess to the Lord whatever sin may be in your life. Always ask the Holy Spirit to reveal
those unrealized sins, the ones that fly beneath our spiritual
radar. Prayerfully ask the Holy Spirit to show you the areas in
your life where changes are required. Make a written list of the
things He shows you. Then agree with the Lord about the nature
of the items on your list: They are sins. Accept the forgiveness
you have received through Christ's death on the cross.

Then as an act of your will, make a choice not to continue
these unhealthy patterns in the future. This is called repentance—learning and turning from an individual sin or a sinful
pattern in your life. Ask the Holy Spirit to enable you to fulfill

your new commitments. The Bible states this wonderful promise: "If we confess our sins to him, he is faithful and just to forgive us and to cleanse us from every wrong" (1 John 1:9). Every sin that you and I have ever committed and will ever commit has been paid for with the precious blood of our Savior. Jesus canceled all the charges against us. We are forgiven for all time. (Now, as a symbolic act, destroy your list of sins. God has forgiven and forgotten them, and so can you!)

HOLD NOTHING BACK

Third, we must surrender control of every area of our lives to our Lord Jesus Christ. For most Christians, this is usually the major obstacle. There is always some area of their lives that they are unwilling to turn over to Christ's rule. It may be finances, relationships, work, friends, or something else. But it is usually

Are you thirsty to know Jesus in a deeper, more meaningful way?

something that they feel they cannot possibly give up. That area will keep them from knowing the sweet joy, peace, and excitement of being totally surrendered to our Lord.

Contemplate the words of the apostle Paul as he admonished the believers in Rome to give themselves completely to the Lord:

And so, dear brothers and sisters, I plead with you to give your bodies to God. Let them be a living and holy sacrifice—the kind he will accept. When you think of what he has done for you, is this too much to ask? Don't copy the behavior and customs of this world, but let God transform you into a new person by changing the way you think. Then you will know what God wants you to do, and you will know how good and pleasing and perfect his will really is.

ROMANS 12:1–2

The very God who created and controls more than one hundred billion galaxies and all they contain is the very One who loved you and me when we were dead in our sins. He loved us enough to send His Son to Earth as a human being, conceived by the Holy Spirit and born of the Virgin Mary, to be crucified for us. You can trust Him with every area of your life.

—❖—

Ask yourself: Do I trust God with the whole picture?

So ask yourself: *Do I trust Him with the whole picture—with every aspect of my life?* Think about each of the major areas of life: work, goals, family, relationships, habits. Which is the hardest for you to entrust to God? The more you truly know Him, the more you will understand that you can trust Him with everything.

GIVE HIM THE THRONE

Fourth, we must ask God to fill us with the Holy Spirit. If you have let go of all the areas of life you were withholding from God and if you have surrendered complete control to Him, then simply ask the Holy Spirit to fill you, to take control of the throne of your life. You can thank God, by faith in His promises, for filling you with His precious Spirit.

Just as you were saved by faith, you will be filled by faith. By faith you will live in His presence and power moment by moment. Salvation was made available to you by your simple, childlike faith in what Christ did for you on the cross. At that time the Holy Spirit came to dwell within you. Being filled by the Spirit works much the same way: As you surrender to Him, He will gladly take control. You simply trust the Spirit to keep His promise.

So many wonderful things will begin to happen in your life after that moment. You will know Jesus Christ as you have never known Him before. You will begin to discover His exciting and challenging will for your life. And because it is what He has created you to do, you will be eager and happy to fulfill it. You will experience the intense joy of fellowship with Him every single day, wherever you go and in whatever you do. You will wonder why you did not allow the Spirit to guide and control your life long, long ago.

If you are not confident that you are filled with the Spirit, I cannot imagine any excuse you might have for delaying another instant. I suggest that you use the following prayer as a guide to help you surrender totally to God:

Dear Father,

I need You. I acknowledge that my life has been a hopeless pattern of sin and disobedience against the loving plan You had for me all along. I thank You and praise You for forgiving my sins through Christ's death on the cross for me. And now, at this watershed moment of my life, I invite Christ to again take His rightful place of authority on the throne of my life. Nothing will be held back. I give it all to You. Fill me with the Holy Spirit as You commanded me to be filled, and as You promised in Your Word that You would do if I asked in faith. I now thank You for directing my life and transforming me into the kind of person You created me to be. Amen.

ENJOY!

From this day forward, you can expect the Holy Spirit to work in and through you—regardless of how you may feel. If you have met the above conditions and have, by faith, asked the Holy Spirit to fill you, rejoice! The work has been done. Now you can expect the Spirit to work in and through you, even if you feel nothing special. Remember that your *FAITH* is not in your *FEELINGS*; rather, your faith is in the *FACT* of God's Word to you. He keeps His promises! You can live with that happy and hopeful expectation at all times, especially in times of adversity.

At times you may feel as if you are bursting with the love and joy of the Holy Spirit. But there may also be times when you feel as if you are in the lowest valley. If so, you may wonder if the Holy Spirit is on vacation—or if all this business about His filling was just your imagination in the first place. Take comfort—these are simply the ups and downs of our moods. Regardless of how we feel, God is working out His perfect will in us and through us whenever we allow Him to do so.

By the power of the Holy Spirit, God is molding His children into the likeness of His Son. Each day that goes by, we should endeavor to be more like Christ and less like our old, sinful natures. You can expect to experience a growing pattern of victories as you face trials and struggles through Christ's strength.

You can expect to feel more peace as you are confronted by crises.

You can expect to feel more peace as you are confronted by crises. As He fills your life, the Holy Spirit will teach you, comfort you, and redirect you toward higher and higher levels where you can be of ever greater service to God. The powerful temptations of today will become easier for you to withstand as you walk hand-in-hand with God through His Spirit in your life.

The Holy Spirit impacts with great blessing every person, church, or family He inhabits and controls. Being filled with the Spirit is an ongoing experience that brings unspeakable joy and delight to the human soul. Expect to see your life change in remarkable ways as you are empowered and guided by the presence of God's Comforter.

LIVE WITH POWER

In the first chapters of this book we have explored essential facts about the Holy Spirit and discussed how you, as a believer in Jesus Christ, can be absolutely certain you are filled with the Spirit of God. The rest of our journey together in this book will demonstrate a number of exciting ways the Spirit will minister to you. As you learn about each of the wonderful ministries of the Holy Spirit, I know you will be eager to surrender greater control of your life to the One who came to glorify Christ and lead us into all truth.

You will want more of His comfort, more of His guidance and teaching, and more of His power in your Christian walk and in your ministry to those around you. The Bible tells us that God has been waiting since the foundation of the universe to unfold the wonderful plans He has for you, and through the power of the Holy Spirit you can know and embrace those plans.

I pray that God will use the chapters that follow to draw you closer to himself, to fill you with His Spirit, and to initiate in you an outreach to others that will influence the world for Christ.

No teaching is more practical than God's teaching.

6

Your Teacher of Truth

If you have ever visited a carnival fun house, perhaps you found yourself wandering into a hall of mirrors. On every wall is a mirror, but those mirrors are sloped, twisted, and angled to create distorted reflections.

While the hall of mirrors might be an amusing place to visit, I think we would all agree that we would rather not live there. Unfortunately, our world is more like that than we would like to admit, because since the fall, sin has twisted and distorted everything. On the day Adam and Eve rebelled against God in the Garden of Eden, sin first made its way into the world. It has done its work of destruction ever since.

We might describe sin as the force that twists all the "mirrors" out of shape. It shows us only grotesque views of what God created to be beautiful. Sin has corrupted everything. We have no fixed point of reference by which to judge anything.

Unless …

Unless we can somehow see life from a godly, biblical perspective. And helping us view life from God's perspective is one role of the Holy Spirit. In this world, we cannot trust our own impressions. We need discernment. We need wisdom. We need a dependable authority. So the Holy Spirit whispers in our ears. If we can learn to hear His voice, we will have a Guide who never fails.

MAKING SENSE OF GOD'S WORD

O ur only safe harbor from untruth is the timeless truth of the Word of God. If we stray away from it, we will quickly fall prey to the world's delusions.

God has provided the Bible so we can navigate our way through a complex and dangerous world. What a wonderful thing to realize that we have access to the very teachings and principles that guided God's people thousands of years ago—and to know that His Word is eternal and never changes.

> *If we learn to hear His voice, we will have a Guide who never fails.*

The Scriptures give us a thorough picture of God's laws, love, and character, as well as case studies of His way of dealing with people. As the Spirit brings light to these words for your life, you will learn more about God than in any other way.

It is no wonder that nonbelievers are puzzled by our allegiance to the Bible; they have no Holy Spirit living within them to illumine and apply its words to their lives. But Christ sent the Holy Spirit to guide us into all truth. He does that in many ways, but the most basic method is through God's Word. The day you became a Christian, the scales fell from your eyes regarding the Holy Scriptures. Up to that point, you could expect to receive no more blessing from those pages than any other nonbeliever might.

But the day you accepted Christ, all that changed. His Holy

Spirit entered your life and opened your eyes to see into the Scriptures with true understanding. Over and over you will hear believers say, "The words really jumped off the page for me!" It is a living Word that we read and cherish. Time and again the Spirit will use the Word to shed light on the issues of your life.

GUIDING YOU INTO ALL TRUTH

As Jesus dined with the disciples in the Upper Room during that final Passover, He offered them a preview of things to come. He told of the coming of the Spirit, who would continue the work that Jesus had begun:

> "When the Spirit of truth comes, he will guide you into all truth. He will not be presenting his own ideas; he will be telling you what he has heard. He will tell you about the future. He will bring me glory by revealing to you whatever he receives from me."
>
> JOHN 16:13–14

In other words, the Spirit comes with a focused agenda. He reveals God's Word and God's plan to you. He equips you for your future.

How does He impart truth to us? The well-known nineteenth century English pastor Charles Spurgeon suggested three distinct strategies. The Holy Spirit, Spurgeon observed, employs *suggestion, direction,* and *illumination* in order to show us truth.

SUGGESTION

Have you ever had a thought cross your mind out of the blue, one that seemed entirely distinct from your normal thought processes? Such notions could come from almost anywhere, of course, but we need to be aware that the Spirit will often place thoughts into our minds. There might be a sudden, powerful notion to pray for a specific individual. We might find that the perfect words are suddenly in our mouths as we give counsel or share our faith. We may think, *I had no idea I could be that eloquent!* We cannot, of course, but the Spirit can.

> *Jesus has a word for every moment and every issue of your life.*

Obviously, we need to be careful about what we credit to the Holy Spirit. We can certainly be misled about the source of an idea. This is why it is so important to take "every thought captive to the obedience of Christ" (2 Corinthians 10:5 NASB). We need to use discernment and "test the spirits" to be certain that we are correctly recognizing God's voice.

DIRECTION

In *suggestion*, a single thought stands out in the mind as if it appeared from nowhere. But there are other times when a chain of thoughts seems to carefully guide us in the direction that God would desire.

Direction does not involve implanted words but a guided stream of thought. The Holy Spirit often directs our thoughts in a particular line of reasoning, leading us to fresh insight and new understanding of the truth. We smile in the knowledge that God's Spirit has redirected our thinking to just where He wanted it to go.

"'My thoughts are completely different from yours,' says the LORD. 'And my ways are far beyond anything you could imagine. For just as the heavens are higher than the earth, so are my ways higher than your ways and my thoughts higher than your thoughts'" (Isaiah 55:8–9).

ILLUMINATION

Earlier in this chapter we explored the way the Spirit works in our lives in regard to the Holy Scriptures. A good word for that is *illumination*. Who better to interpret the Scriptures for us than the very One who inspired them? The greatest wisdom of the ages seems to make no sense at all unless illumined by the light of the Holy Spirit. Jesus has a word for every day, every moment, and every issue of your life. He will offer it to you through the wonderful ministry of the Holy Spirit.

COOPERATING WITH YOUR TEACHER

The amount you will learn from the Spirit of truth is based not on His performance, for He is available equally and fully to all believers. Rather, what you learn depends on your cooperation and teachableness as His student. The acrostic "TRUTH" will help you remember several keys to cooperating with the Holy Spirit as He teaches you truth.

> "The Spirit teaches you all things, and what he teaches is true."
> —Jesus Christ

T *rust the Holy Spirit to Teach You*
Jesus promised that the Holy Spirit would guide us into all truth. God keeps His promises, so we can put our faith in those promises. If you yield control of the throne of your life to Jesus Christ, you can trust that the Holy Spirit will teach you God's truth. The apostle John offers the highest of recommendations:

But you have received the Holy Spirit, and he lives within you, so you don't need anyone to teach you what is true. For the Spirit teaches you all things, and what he teaches is true—it is not a lie. So continue in what he has taught you, and continue to live in Christ.

1 JOHN 2:27

We would be foolish not to trust the Spirit to teach us. And we would be unwise to not be the best possible students. I challenge you to ask the Spirit of truth to teach you all that He has for you. Dedicate yourself to listening, learning, then living.

Revel in God's Truth

A great deal of what the Holy Spirit has for you to learn has already been recorded in the Scriptures. Thus you'll want to be diligent in regular, frequent study of God's Word. So powerful will be its positive impact in your life that, in time, you will not be able to imagine going more than a day without it.

Make sure that you have a worthy translation of the Scriptures, one with good study notes. Keep a notebook with your Bible so you can write down all you learn as it comes to you. Underscore passages that you sense the Spirit may be underscoring in your heart.

I heartily recommend that you commit to memory key verses that give you assurance of your salvation, insight into God's love and majesty, strength against temptation, and guidance for living a life that pleases your heavenly Father. Often we are hesitant to do this kind of work, excusing ourselves for being "lousy at memorization," but how is it that we can memorize names, faces, numbers, sports and movie trivia, and other details of life? What could possibly be more worth memorizing than the promises and teaching of God himself? An investment of a few minutes each day to memorize a verse of Scripture will pay handsome spiritual dividends for the rest of your life. The Spirit will fill your heart and mind with the Word of God wherever you may go. Your life will be wonderfully enriched when the Word becomes the soundtrack of your life.

Even at eighty years of age, I'm still memorizing Scripture and reveling in passages that I memorized more than fifty years ago. There is no material treasure that can compare with the Scripture you hold securely in your heart.

*U*ncover Truth by Meditating on God's Word

We are more accustomed to reading for information. That is important, but we also need to take time to let the Word simply soak into our hearts and minds.

There is an art to meditating on the Word of God, and it takes some time to cultivate such an art. Reflection and meditation go much deeper than the kind of reading most of us do. We must attempt to dig deeply into the Scripture passage, understand it as thoroughly as possible, and discover what the Spirit might be saying to us through it. Be inquisitive! As you reflect on a passage, ask questions such as these:

- What does it say?
- Is there a command for me to follow?
- Is there a promise for me to claim?

Listen for the Holy Spirit's application of the passage to your life. Take your time and don't be impatient. Be sensitive to what He is saying and to His instruction. He may illuminate a verse so that it suddenly comes alive and seems to jump off the page into your heart as never before.

He may also provide a whole new understanding of a passage that you have read many times. So resist the natural inclination to think, *Yes, I have read this verse before so I'll move on.* The Bible is supernatural. What didn't stand out to you yesterday may come alive to you today. Listen anew for what the verse says about your life here and now.

*T*est Insights to Be Certain They Are from God

This is a point we must never forget. Many terrible delusions have come from misapplication of Scripture. How can we know that we are hearing the voice of the Holy Spirit—the only Spirit of truth—and not some other voice? I suggest that you test insights with the following questions:

1. *Are your impressions consistent with Scripture?* The Holy Spirit will never guide you to act in a manner that is in conflict with Scripture. The more you learn about God's Word, the more you will be impressed with the consistency of the scriptural message.

———————❖———————

How can we know that we are hearing the Spirit's voice?

———————

2. *Does the insight make sense?* Satan suggested to Jesus that He jump off the highest point of the temple in order to let the angels catch Him. Jesus knew His mission, and common sense indicated that this was not part of it. There are some decisions in life that you will not need to pray about. The common sense that God gave you, controlled by the Holy Spirit, should be sufficient to help you make wise decisions.

3. *Is the insight sensible in the light of circumstances?* If you are deeply in debt but you want to buy an expensive new car, it is unlikely that God is the one telling you to make the

purchase. The Scriptures make clear that He is not a God of disorder or irrationality.

4. *Do godly pastors, teachers, and counselors agree with the impressions you have received?* It is important to seek wise counsel. Surround yourselves with wise, mature believers who will provide a spiritual "safety net" to help protect you from a poor interpretation of God's will.

5. *Does the insight you have received generate deep inner peace?* This is the kind of peace the world simply cannot give. Running away from our circumstances may generate some peace—but only for a time. The kind of peace I am speaking of is not dependent on your circumstances. It is the supernatural peace that comes directly from God and overrides whatever circumstances you face. If you are unsure of your interpretation and application of the Scriptures, look into your heart and determine whether you are experiencing the peace that comes from God.

*H*asten to Apply God's Truth to Your Life

No teaching is more practical than God's teaching, and this realization should spur you to listen even more attentively. When you learn something, you will usually see, quickly enough, the reason the Spirit taught it to you.

In the long run, of course, learning from the Spirit makes a difference in your life only if you act upon what you have learned. He teaches you not so that you will have more information, but so that you will have more impact.

GOD IS WORKING IN YOU, GIVING YOU THE DESIRE TO OBEY
HIM AND THE POWER TO DO WHAT PLEASES HIM.

PHILIPPIANS 2:13

7

Your Helper in Prayer

Envision the scene that opens Luke 11. Jesus is caught up in deep prayer, barely conscious of the disciples who have gathered to watch Him with fascination.

Imagine what those disciples saw, heard, and felt. Here was a man praying as no one had ever been seen or heard to pray. In those days, the Pharisees offered prayers that were public, pompous, and predictable. Prayer was a "town square" demonstration of one's religiosity. It was also one-way communication, for God seemed silent during this period (He had not spoken powerfully since the time of the prophets). For most, prayer had become an empty, meaningless exercise.

But here was Jesus, who prayed at all times. He slipped away each morning for prayer, sought God in the midst of each important development, and seemed to have an incredible intimacy with His Father. His kind of prayer was nothing like the "vain repetition" of the Pharisees; it more resembled a meeting with a beloved friend.

So the disciples watched with wonder as He prayed. One of them could no longer contain his desire to experience something so wonderful. As soon as Jesus finished praying, the disciple cried out, "Lord, teach us to pray!"

TALKING *WITH* GOD, NOT *TO* GOD

Have you ever felt like that disciple, longing to know how to pray? Perhaps you have commiserated with Ziggy, the cartoon character who stood on the mountain peak and called out to heaven, "Am I to be put on hold for the rest of my life?" All of us feel a deep craving not simply to talk *to* God, but to talk *with* God. We have no desire for the mere trappings of prayer; we want the real thing. And each of us has felt the disappointment of dry, dead prayer in which our words seem to bounce off the ceiling and return to us unheard.

We read books on the subject. We try new methods. We wonder if there is some hidden formula or secret that will provide the key to powerful prayer. But in reality there is only one secret—His name is the Holy Spirit. He carries us beyond our weaknesses and limitations. He carries us directly into the incredible, loving presence of God himself.

Prayer is the most intimate communication ever devised. It is heart-to-heart, spirit-to-Spirit communication between creation and Creator.

Prayer is:

talking with God,

asking Him for guidance,

listening for His answers,

praising Him for His goodness,

confessing our shortcomings,

sharing with Him the needs of ourselves and others, and

knowing by faith that He hears us, He cares, and He grants
    our needs.

GETTING BEYOND THE CURTAIN

In the days when the temple was still in use in Jerusalem, only the high priest was allowed to enter the Holy of Holies to atone for the sins of the people—and this only once a year. When he entered that sacred place, he came into the very presence of God. An individual's closest encounter with God would be to interact with the priest, and on the public side of the curtain.

But as believers in Jesus Christ, we can now go beyond the curtain. We can approach the eternal, infinite Creator God of the universe any time of the day, any day of the year. Why? Because of the selfless sacrifice of our Savior Jesus when He died on the cross for our sins, we can "boldly enter heaven's Most Holy Place" (Hebrews 10:19).

The Spirit is the one who eagerly clasps your hand and walks you into God's throne room. "Now all of us, both Jews and Gentiles, may come to the Father through the same Holy Spirit because of what Christ has done for us" (Ephesians 2:18).

We should look upon prayer as the most precious, valuable privilege we could ever receive. We should take advantage of it at every available instant, and with eagerness: "So let us come boldly to the throne of our gracious God. There we will receive his mercy, and we will find grace to help us when we need it" (Hebrews 4:16).

As our helper in prayer, the Spirit does a number of wonderful things to enrich our prayer life.

THE SPIRIT PROMPTS YOU TO PRAY

Have you ever felt that little nudge? You may be going about your business, your mind on many earthly matters, when you sense a little mental tug. You feel the urge to pray about a particular matter or person. This impression could even wake you

in the middle of the night. We hear of many Christians who, in
various situations, were led to pray for a loved one or friend,
only to find that this person was in a dangerous situation at that
very moment.

THE SPIRIT GUIDES YOUR PRAYERS

The Holy Spirit also molds and shapes our prayers, helping
them to be effective and consistent with the will of God. He
guides us through the needs of the day, through the emotions
of the hour, and through recollections of people we care about.
He helps us pray for all the many things we need to bring
before the Father.

As He does this, something wonderful happens. The Spirit
brings our desires into conformity with God's will. It may be
that you have encountered a very difficult situation in life. You
feel a great deal of anxiety, and naturally you ask God for a
change in the circumstances. But as the days and prayers move
by, you find that the circumstances remain the same while your
attitude has utterly changed: You suddenly comprehend how
God could use someone like you in just such a setting. You
realize that He did not want to help you out of this mess but to
help you *through* it. More miracles happen in the midst of
crises than when we are fleeing from our circumstances.

God's Spirit guides your prayer over time, until you find
yourself asking Him to *lead you through* rather than *remove
you from* the situation. The Bible assures us, "God is working
in you, giving you the desire to obey him and the power to do
what pleases him" (Philippians 2:13).

You pray for God to change things, but in the process you
are the one changed. It works much like the anchor on a ship.
When men take hold of the chain to the anchor, their efforts

pull the boat toward the anchor, rather than the anchor up to the boat. In the same way, when we pray, tugging at the "chain" of prayer pulls us toward God. We are moved gradually into His awesome presence where our hearts are transformed by the power of His love.

Prayer keeps you anchored in every sense of the word. When you feel the pull of the Spirit to turn your heart toward prayer, you can be joyful in realizing that you will be even closer to the wonderful purposes of God by the time you have finished. The Spirit guides our prayer, and best of all He guides our spirits toward God.

THE SPIRIT INTERCEDES FOR YOU

Here is one of the most remarkable promises and supernatural ministries of the Spirit in prayer: "In the same way, the Spirit helps us in our weakness. We do not know what we ought to pray for, but the Spirit himself intercedes for us with groans that words cannot express" (Romans 8:26 NIV).

I have always found this to be a tremendously encouraging concept. You may say, "But I don't know how to pray!" Every believer should learn to pray biblically, following the model Jesus gave us in what we call the Lord's Prayer. However, that is not the major issue, because the Spirit prays for those things we lack the understanding to pray for. He also expresses the depth of emotion that we might feel if we could see with complete spiritual clarity. He helps us pray beyond our many limitations. Knowing this makes me all the more eager to pray, as I am sure it does you.

The Holy Spirit knows us better than we know ourselves. He understands our desires, our fears, our strengths, and our weaknesses. He knows what we need before we even know to ask for it. The Holy Spirit, the third Person of the Trinity, knows the mind of God. "He who searches our hearts knows the mind of the Spirit, because the Spirit intercedes for the saints in accordance with God's will" (Romans 8:27 NIV).

Who better to speak to our heavenly Father for us than the Holy Spirit?

We have so many limitations, so many failings. But we can be joyful knowing that the Spirit of God stands in the gap, interceding for us. Your prayers are more powerful than you can possibly realize because He enhances and enlarges them.

THE SPIRIT LEADS YOU IN PRAYERFUL WORSHIP

Prayer, of course, is more than a flood of requests. The Holy Spirit helps us praise and exalt God when we pray. He helps us realize the awesomeness of God. He helps us comprehend just how infinite, how majestic, and how sovereign He truly is. As a result, we can do nothing other than worship God in spirit and in truth.

COOPERATING WITH YOUR PRAYER HELPER

We have seen but a mere sampling of how the Holy Spirit helps us in prayer. But how can we be caught up in the kind of prayer that allows us to sense the transforming presence of God? Let me offer three ways you can cooperate with the Holy Spirit as He helps you pray.

ADDRESS GOD RESPECTFULLY

To pray in the Spirit is to pray with a reverent heart. We should never come before God without reverence and awe. "Since we are receiving a kingdom that cannot be destroyed, let us be thankful and please God by worshiping him with holy fear and awe" (Hebrews 12:28).

Fear is a word that is often missing today from our understanding of a relationship with God, but I believe it refers to a surpassing sense of how awesome and holy God is.

BE TRANSPARENT WITH GOD

Praying as the Spirit leads also gives us the freedom to be ourselves. As we have seen in James 5:16, "The effective prayer of a *righteous* man can accomplish much" (NASB). If we have confessed our sin, we realize there is no obstacle between God and us. We can be completely open and honest, telling Him exactly what is on our hearts. "If our conscience is clear, we can come to God with bold confidence. And we will receive whatever we request because we obey him and do the things that please him" (1 John 3:21–22). The key to answered prayer, then, is being in harmony with God. As we come into His presence and know Him more fully, that harmony grows.

No relationship can be deep and strong without honest communication, and your relationship with God is no different. Wonderful liberation is experienced when we learn what it is like to be completely honest with God, with no shame or striving to be something we are not. We can worship Him "in spirit and in truth," as Jesus told the woman at the well (John 4:23). When you pray in the Spirit, you will be transparent with God. He knows all that is inside you anyway.

BE CONFIDENT IN GOD

While we need to approach God in reverence and awe, there is no need to come before God with hesitation and timidity, as if we lack trust in His power. We are praying to the Creator and Sustainer of the universe. If we are praying as the Spirit directs, we can confidently come before Him with our requests.

This means fully realizing our dependence upon Him. One of the most essential effects of prayer is that it reminds us how helpless we are apart from God. Each day we must submit ourselves to His lordship again, because our spirits are rebellious and stubborn. As we come before God, we acknowledge our limitations. We cast ourselves upon His mercy and His power, affirming that we can do no good thing on our own.

Then, having felt our own helplessness, we express faith in His worthiness. Praying as the Spirit directs strengthens our faith that though we are weak, He is strong. As we pray, we *believe*—we believe He will act as He desires. We believe He will work through us. We believe He is totally sovereign. Faith is strengthened when we pray in the Spirit and we begin to live in the confident assurance that He is Lord, and that He is working in our world and through us. Praying in the power of the Holy Spirit always leads to greater confidence and hope in God.

In the matter of prayer, perseverance counts. Faith that God will act is not the same as faith that God will act today, tomorrow, or whatever our timetable may be. He wants us to pray without ceasing, to keep praying with persistence. He knows that the discipline of sustained prayer is good for us.

We do not serve a God of convenience but a God of perfect timing—a timing we usually will not know in advance. Keep on keeping on as you pray in the Spirit with faith and endurance. Never give up!

8

Your Motivator to Holiness

At the beginning of the nineteenth-century lived a sculptor named Dannecker, one of the finest artists in the world. He specialized in carving images of Greek gods and goddesses. But Dannecker wanted to produce a true masterpiece—and he set his mind on sculpting a figure of the Christ.

Dannecker's finished work was so beautiful that it brought gasps of admiration from everyone who saw it. Eventually, word of the new masterpiece reached the ears of the emperor Napoleon. "Come to Paris," he invited, through a message to the artist. "Carve me a statue of Venus for the Louvre."

The sculptor Dannecker politely replied, "Sir, the hands that carved the Christ can never again carve a heathen goddess."

Once the power of the Holy Spirit has opened our eyes to really see Jesus, we are spoiled for anything else; we actually want to live a life that is clean, pure, and holy. The Holy Spirit helps us see God and, consequently, to see everything else differently.

We must do our work for God in the darkness of this world. But while we are *in* the world, we can never again be a part *of* the world. There are harmful activities we must leave behind, habits we must break, and relationships we can no longer pursue. We know that our God has standards much higher than those of the world and that our lives must begin to conform to them as closely as possible.

The Lord says to us, "You must be holy because I am holy" (1 Peter 1:16). Those words, of course, are intimidating to us, for we are prone to sin and failure. How can we attain a holiness worthy of God? This is why Jesus came to die for us, even when we were yet sinners—because we had no hope of becoming worthy on our own. Yet the scriptural command remains consistent and clear: We must be holy. We must lead lives of purity.

It seems a paradox, but we know our Lord would never give a command without affording us the provision for keeping it. How can we live in purity while we are surrounded by so much sin and temptation? The answer: the Holy Spirit, our Motivator and Guide to holy living.

OLD HABITS DIE HARD

Few believers realize how many spiritual events occur in that incredible instant when we invite Christ to be our Savior.

First and foremost, we are liberated from Satan's grasp and reconciled to God. The Bible explains, "For he has rescued us out of the darkness and gloom of Satan's kingdom and brought us into the Kingdom of his dear Son, who bought our freedom with his blood and forgave us all our sins" (Colossians 1:13–14 TLB).

Second, we become brand-new creatures. Paul tells us this marvelous truth: "If anyone is in Christ, he is a new creation; the old has gone, the new has come!" (2 Corinthians 5:17 NIV). It is like wiping the slate clean and starting life all over again—in complete purity. All the perfection of Christ is attributed to us, though we do not merit this in the least. The Bible declares, "You were washed, you were sanctified, you were justified in the name of the Lord Jesus Christ and by the Spirit of our God" (1 Corinthians 6:11 NIV).

But here is a crucial point: Though these wonderful things have happened and though we have been made completely new, we are still human beings with free will. We can still choose to listen to the destructive influence of the old self.

God would never give a command without giving us the provision for keeping it.

Our lives do not immediately become beautiful, problem-free, and exempt from sin at the moment Christ comes to indwell us. Thus the Holy Spirit is about His work, strengthening and sanctifying us to bring us closer and closer to the image of Christ.

Those old habits die hard. The voice of the Devil will still be in our ear, whispering enticements to do things the old, sinful way. (Remember, the flesh is constantly at war with God.)

Throughout my Christian life, as I have faced temptations of many kinds, I have claimed the promise of 1 Corinthians 10:13: "No temptation has seized you except what is common to man. And God is faithful; he will not let you be tempted beyond what you can bear. But when you are tempted, he will also provide a way out so that you can stand up under it" (NIV).

This promise is available to each of us in the war against sin. We are in a daily battle, and through our victories over temptation we will become stronger, wiser, and more holy.

As you grow in Christ, you will want a new kind of life that reflects Him at its center. Everything in your life should point back to Him. You will be painfully aware of issues such as how you interact with people, what kinds of books and films and Web sites you select, what kind of thoughts you nurture, and how you spend your time. The Holy Spirit will show you everything in a new light. He will prod you to make positive changes and He will give you the supernatural power to make those changes. You will undergo a work of daily renewal and renovation, but I can assure you that it is a satisfying work when you let the Holy Spirit do the reconstructing. You will be pleased with the new, upgraded life that results.

Take to heart the wonderful benediction Paul pronounces over you, God's cherished creation: "Now may the God of peace make you holy in every way, and may your whole spirit and soul and body be kept blameless until that day when our Lord Jesus Christ comes again. God, who calls you, is faithful; he will do this" (1 Thessalonians 5:23–24).

WHY DO WE CONTINUE TO SIN?

There is everything to gain and only sorrow to lose when you live moment by moment in the purity of holiness. The choice is so clear. Yet, so many believers fail the test day after day, choice after choice. Why is this so?

For one thing, we make the mistake of attempting to live in purity through our own weak abilities and self-effort. It takes a supernatural enabling to live in constant victory when we are surrounded by the lure and temptations of the world.

That ability is available only through the Holy Spirit. Paul wrote, "Let me ask you this one question: Did you receive the Holy Spirit by keeping the law? Of course not, for the Holy Spirit came upon you only after you believed the message you heard about Christ. Have you lost your senses? After starting your Christian lives in the Spirit, why are you now trying to become perfect by your own human effort?" (Galatians 3:2–3). Our own weakness brought us to God in the first place, and it is a great mistake to continue living in that weakness.

At the same time, many of us sin because we fail to realize our true nature. Let this verse saturate your mind: "Our old sinful selves were crucified with Christ so that sin might lose its power in our lives. We are no longer slaves to sin. For when we died with Christ we were set free from the power of sin" (Romans 6:6–7). After the American Civil War, all slavery was outlawed. Those who had lived as slaves were completely free. But tragically, there were many who were not told. They continued to live and toil in bondage because they had no knowledge that a new life was possible. We, too, often fail to realize the truth of our emancipation. Christ has truly set us free. We need not live in servitude to Satan. The time has come to shake off the chains and begin a new life.

There is also the problem of simply giving in to the desires of the old sin nature. We fall into those old sinful patterns. Paul explains the impulses that still sadly control some of us:

> I advise you to live according to your new life in the Holy
> Spirit. Then you won't be doing what your sinful nature
> craves. The old sinful nature loves to do evil, which is
> just opposite from what the Holy Spirit wants. And the
> Spirit gives us desires that are opposite from what the

sinful nature desires. These two forces are constantly fighting each other, and your choices are never free from this conflict.

GALATIANS 5:16–17

The Devil, of course, is always at work through the world and the old sin nature that is still within us. We should never forget that he will use every clever strategy to make the world and its sin seem attractive. Because each day is fraught with temptations that he will place in our paths, we need to daily put on our spiritual armor and stand firm. Every believer should regularly meditate on the sixth chapter of Ephesians, especially the following portion:

> Be strong with the Lord's mighty power. Put on all of God's armor so that you will be able to stand firm against all strategies and tricks of the Devil. For we are not fighting against people made of flesh and blood, but against the evil rulers and authorities of the unseen world, against those mighty powers of darkness who rule this world, and against wicked spirits in the heavenly realms.

EPHESIANS 6:10–12

There is one other but very crucial reason why we continue to sin. We lack a reverential fear of God. If we truly comprehended the greatness and sovereignty of God, if we understood His absolute purity and holiness, if we could grasp how He abhors and punishes sin, we could not possibly remain stubborn in our disobedience.

Our God is loving and full of grace. He is gentle and forgiving. But it is equally true that "our God is a consuming fire" (Hebrews 12:29) and that "it is a terrible thing to fall into the hands of the living God" (Hebrews 10:31). The Creator and Sustainer of the universe has the power to give life or to snatch it away. Life is fragile, like a mist, and we owe every breath to Him. We need to realize that He must, as a part of His just and holy nature, punish sin for what it is: an affront to His purity.

HOW THEN SHALL WE LIVE?

To live for self is to be consumed with self-absorption. It will set us immediately at odds not only with God but with all other people, including ourselves. We will be led to break God's laws and to break ourselves upon them. Only misery, sorrow, and tragedy can result.

However, living for Christ will place us under the influence of the Spirit of God, who will guide us with love and grace. We will live to please Him and others,

> *To live for self is to be consumed with self-absorption.*

therefore finding wonderful fulfillment and peace for ourselves. In the meantime, we will be constantly about the work of purification, keeping our lives as clean vessels for the shining presence of God. Paul encourages us, "Let us purify ourselves from everything that contaminates body and spirit, perfecting holiness out of reverence for God" (2 Corinthians 7:1 NIV).

You may not feel righteous. You may think God still condemns you for past sin. But in truth, you have been freed from sin and death by Christ's own death on the cross. The Spirit of God lives within you. When the Father looks at you, He sees all the righteousness of His dearly beloved Son. "God made him who had no sin to be sin for us, so that in him we might become the righteousness of God" (2 Corinthians 5:21 NIV).

Since Christ was put to death for you, you must put your old self to death for Him. "Those who belong to Christ Jesus have nailed the passions and desires of their sinful nature to his cross and crucified them there" (Galatians 5:24). God wants us to crucify the old, corrupted person we once were.

Forgiveness and salvation come once, but the execution of the sinful nature is a daily, moment-by-moment event. We need the Holy Spirit to give us strength, wisdom, and resolve in continuing to experience victory over the old sin nature that once controlled us. It would rise yet again from its grave and regain control over us, but the presence of the Spirit provides all the power we need to resist yielding to temptation.

This Is Only a Test

Temptation may seem severe, but it is only a test. The Lord will never allow Satan to tempt you beyond what you are able to endure. He will always provide you with a way out. The Bible promises, "So humble yourselves before God. Resist the Devil, and he will flee from you" (James 4:7).

Paul counsels us to immerse our minds in all that is worthy: "Fix your thoughts on what is true and honorable and right. Think about things that are pure and lovely and admirable. Think about things that are excellent and worthy of praise" (Philippians 4:8). We are surrounded, however, by the very opposite. Many television shows, movies, magazines, and Web sites will fix your thoughts on much that is false and dishonorable.

It is an essential Christian discipline to control the environment of your imagination. Your thoughts and values change when exposed to pornography, violence, and other sinful activities. Even spending time with cynical, sarcastic people will affect your perspective. Advertisers spend billions of dollars each year on the proposition that images and sensory information can change your mind and behavior. Because we know this is true, we must strive to expose ourselves to good and worthy influences at every turn. Take care what you allow into your mind.

Let God's Spirit empower you daily to walk in all of His ways. Ask Him to guide you moment by moment and to keep you from evil.

Live by the Spirit, and you will not gratify the desires of the sinful nature. (Galatians 5:16 NIV)

Scripture assures us, "Live by the Spirit, and you will not gratify the desires of the sinful nature" (Galatians 5:16 NIV). Ask Him to show you the impurities that need to be cleaned away, as well as any obstacles to the holy and pleasing life He would like you to lead. Ask Him to strengthen you for a new life today—a life pure and powerful in its commitment to God's standards.

———————— ❖ ————————

GOD IS NOT ONLY WITH US IN OUR TRIALS,
BUT HE IS ALSO REFINING US THROUGH THEM.

————————————————

9

Your Comforter in Adversity

et's face it: Life is difficult. It can be unpredictable, challenging, and often brutal.

We shake our heads as we watch innocent people suffer and dishonest people prosper. The world does not seem to play by the rules of fairness and justice. I am certain that somewhere on the road of your own experience, you have discovered this truth in the most painful ways. We can only rest in the assurance that God has a purpose for all the adversity He allows in our lives.

At our lowest points, we can be reminded that suffering refines our character. There are things we cannot learn, virtues we cannot gain, through any path other than the crucible of suffering. As we have all observed, young children must learn certain things the hard way. We can tell them what is right and what is wrong, but there is no more powerful teacher than experience. Life works the same way, on a different level, for the rest of us. We need to learn patience, and we can learn it only through the agony of waiting. We need to learn forgiveness, and we can develop it only when there is something difficult to forgive.

Suffering is never welcome, but it is nearly always useful. When we undergo some painful affliction in life, our first question is usually, "Why me?" I would suggest to you that this is the wrong question. A better one would be, "What is God trying to teach me?" We will never know why bad things happen, but we can discover what good things can emerge from them. Affliction is often the messenger of God's deepest truths. And in the midst of our struggles the Holy Spirit reminds us that we are not alone—God is not only with us in our trials, but He is also refining us through them.

A TIME FOR JOY

When any kind of fine metal is being refined, impurities must be burned away. When we feel pain in life, we can look upon it as our own period of refinement. We can remember that we are on the way to becoming God's pure and strong metal, ready to serve Him. There is a purpose to our suffering as long as we keep our eyes on Him. Without the Holy Spirit's comfort, we suffer alone and without hope. But with the Holy Spirit, we can go beyond patience and acceptance—the Bible tells us that suffering is an opportunity for nothing less than joy:

> Dear brothers and sisters, whenever trouble comes your way, let it be an opportunity for joy. For when your faith is tested, your endurance has a chance to grow. So let it grow, for when your endurance is fully developed, you will be strong in character and ready for anything.
>
> JAMES 1:2–4

Have you ever looked upon trouble as a time for joy? This is not foolishness but the deepest kind of wisdom. This joyful perspective is the very key to persevering and growing in wisdom during times of affliction. We regard a problem not as a stumbling block

---❖---

Suffering is never welcome but it is nearly always useful.

---

lem not as a stumbling block but as a stepping-stone. This is a necessary stop on the way to a life that is useful to God. It is the way to deeper understanding through the fires of experience. It is the way to learning to comfort and counsel others. Tears may come, but they should be tears not only of pain but also of hard-won joy.

Listen to what God said to Israel through the prophet Isaiah:

> When you go through deep waters and great trouble, I
> will be with you. When you go through rivers of difficulty,
> you will not drown! When you walk through the fire of
> oppression, you will not be burned up; the flames will not
> consume you.
>
> ISAIAH 43:2

Our loving God is so creative and resourceful. Where we see limitations, He sees unlimited opportunity. He finds great joy in bringing the greatest miracles from the harshest conditions.

The disciples must have trembled in fear in that Upper Room as Jesus told them He would be leaving. What would life be like without the Master? Yet Jesus assured them that He would not leave them alone; He would send them a Comforter. The word He used is translated as "comforter, counselor, encourager." It has the meaning of someone who is called alongside to help in times of trouble.

The Holy Spirit is the One who comes to us with tender comfort and encouragement as well as power and strength. He is the ideal companion when we are beset by misery and grief. He knows us deeply, intimately, better than we know ourselves. He knows exactly what kind of encouragement we need, and He has the power to strengthen and heal us. In times when we feel incapable of expressing the depth of our pain, we can know that He understands.

The woman slowly opened her hands to reveal broken, beaten fingers.

It is a wonderful truth to contemplate: We need never again be alone. Where could you go to escape the companionship of the Holy Spirit? What pain could you feel that He would not understand and comfort? I hope you will remember that wherever you are, whatever trial you may face, the Comforter is right there beside you.

NO GREATER LOVE

Perhaps you remember the film *The Hiding Place* from some years ago. The book and the film tell the story of my dear friend Corrie ten Boom and her sister, Betsie, who were sent to Ravensbrück concentration camp during World War II because they had protected Jewish people.

One night several women gathered around Betsie as she led a Bible study. One of the prisoners suddenly spoke bitterly, "If your God is such a good God, why does He allow this kind of suffering?" The woman slowly opened her hands to reveal broken, beaten fingers. "I am the first violinist of the symphony orchestra. Did your God will *this*?"

Corrie looked sadly at the woman's hands. "We can't answer that question," she said with compassion. "All we know is that our God came to this earth, became one of us, suffered with us, and was crucified and died. And He did it for love."

God's love for us is deep and personal. Through His Spirit, He enters into the places of our pain and performs a work of healing that cannot be matched. Only He is capable of bringing such strength, endurance, and even joy in the face of the worst of calamities.

This incredible power in the face of affliction is not possible through any human agency or reserve, but only through the supernatural power of God's Spirit. He loves us with an everlasting love, and He fills us with an everlasting comfort. The power comes from knowing and living out what Paul wrote to the Romans:

> I am convinced that nothing can ever separate us from his love. Death can't, and life can't. The angels can't, and the demons can't. Our fears for today, our worries about tomorrow, and even the powers of hell can't keep God's love away. Whether we are high above the sky or in the deepest ocean, nothing in all creation will ever be able to separate us from the love of God that is revealed in Christ Jesus our Lord.
>
> ROMANS 8:38 39

They can take away all of our possessions. They can even take away our physical life. But they can never take away the most precious attainment we have, which is our living relationship with God, who loves us unconditionally. To know that is to be empowered for joy!

Life will always have its worries, but we have a place to go with them. The Comforter reminds us that the victory has already been won, and we can face the worst that life has to offer. Jesus said, "Here on earth you will have many trials and sorrows. But take heart, because I have overcome the world" (John 16:33). It does not matter if the entire Roman army is arrayed against us. It does not matter if the powers of Hollywood, Madison Avenue, and Washington, D.C. oppose us. It does not matter if our bosses, coworkers, and neighbors are negative toward Christ. It is only Christ whose opinion matters. He has overcome the world, and He promises believers that all our pain will ultimately be used for our good (Romans 8:28).

COOPERATING WITH THE COMFORTER

The Spirit is your Comforter, and He is always with you in every time of trial or grief. But this comfort is not something to look upon passively. Here are some practical ways you can cooperate with the Holy Spirit and experience His comforting strength in difficult times.

CAST YOUR CARES UPON GOD

The Bible says, "Give all your worries and cares to God, for he cares about what happens to you" (1 Peter 5:7). What a wonderful invitation! The God of the universe, the God who created us, wants us to cast *all* our burdens on Him. Wouldn't it be foolish to ignore His offer and attempt to "gut it out" on our own, without the comfort of God's Spirit?

TURN YOUR EYES OUTWARD

When we face adversity, we can either become self-absorbed and completely focused on our problems, or we can turn our eyes to selfless ministry to others. Paul, in reflecting upon his own suffering, wrote, "I am willing to endure anything if it will bring salvation and eternal glory in Christ Jesus to those God has chosen" (2 Timothy 2:10). You will find in all his letters that as he faced trials and disappointments, Paul turned himself more and more to serving his many friends in the body of Christ. As you face trials, redouble your commitment to serve God in the midst of them.

CLAIM GOD'S PROMISES

Let me underscore once again the power of claiming God's promises. These are the richest and most exciting truths known to humanity, and the best time to reach for them is when you need comfort. I encourage you to memorize as many of God's promises as possible so that the Holy Spirit may bring to your mind the perfect promise at just the time you need it. "Trust me in your times of trouble," says the Lord, "and I will rescue you, and you will give me glory" (Psalm 50:15). That trust will be bolstered by claiming any of the multitude of promises found in the Scriptures. Is there any way the schemes of Satan can be successful in the face of God's power? Not if we claim victory through Christ. Our victory as believers is assured not because of our good works, but because at the cross Jesus Christ triumphed over Satan, the world, and sin. The war itself has been won, and we can face these lingering skirmishes with full assurance. The apostle Paul writes:

> That is why we never give up. Though our bodies are
> dying, our spirits are being renewed every day. For our
> present troubles are quite small and won't last very long.
> Yet they produce for us an immeasurably great glory that

will last forever! So we don't look at the troubles we can see right now; rather, we look forward to what we have not yet seen. For the troubles we see will soon be over, but the joys to come will last forever.

2 CORINTHIANS 4:16–18

LOOK FOR THE GOOD

Hold a coin in your hand and you will agree that you can view only one side at a time. Suffering is a kind of coin that is paid out to everyone. If you are going to view one side, choose the victorious one. Look closely at the side whose inscription reads, "And we know that God causes everything to work together for the good of those who love God and are called according to his purpose for them" (Romans 8:28). Study the image on this side of the coin—the image of Christ that we are coming to resemble more every day through the power of the Spirit and through the wisdom and endurance that comes through our suffering. Hold this coin tightly in your hand, for it will help to purchase a future of maturity and assurance. Paul suffered as much as any of us, and he turned every tear to joy. He wrote these words: "We can rejoice, too, when we run into problems and trials, for we know that they are good for us— they help us learn to endure. And endurance develops strength of character in us, and character strengthens our confident expectation of salvation" (Romans 5:3–4). I believe that if you comprehend this truth, you will learn to face your trials with a positive mindset.

FOCUS ON GOD'S FAITHFULNESS

The Scriptures tell us, "So if you are suffering according to God's will, keep on doing what is right, and trust yourself to the

God who made you, for he will never fail you" (1 Peter 4:19). In other words, put your trust in the faithfulness of God, and obey Him in your actions as you await the victory that will come through adversity.

THANK GOD IN THE MIDST OF YOUR DIFFICULTIES

When times are good, give thanks. When times are bad, give thanks. When times are somewhere in the middle, give thanks! Because Christ lives in us through His Spirit, we are to maintain an attitude of thanksgiving at all times. Paul wrote, "No matter what happens, always be thankful, for this is God's will for you who belong to Christ Jesus" (1 Thessalonians 5:18).

I believe you will find that even during the most difficult trials, there will never be a time when you cannot think of a wide assortment of blessings for which to be thankful. Indeed, the trials themselves present occasions for thanksgiving. We can say, "Thank You, Lord, for the things You will teach me from this experience. Thank You for the wisdom I will store up from the school of suffering. Thank You that, although I do not fully understand why I am facing these hardships, I know without a doubt that You can be trusted, and that everything I encounter will be used for my good."

> *"Thank You, Lord, for the things You will teach me from this experience."*

You will be amazed at how your frame of mind will change simply by thanking God. He will honor you for your steadfast faith. The Holy Spirit will bring you comfort and encouragement and you will feel a "second wind" to keep running the race—and claim victory at the finish line.

OUR CLOTHING, OUR CULTURE, OUR LANGUAGE,
AND OUR CUSTOMS MAY DIFFER, BUT THE LORD WHO
BINDS US TOGETHER IS ONE AND THE SAME.

10

Your Peacemaker in Conflict

A ll around us there are wars and rumors of wars. It has
always been that way and always will be until our Lord
returns.

By now it should be clear that humanity will be at war with
itself as long as we remain at war with God. Only in Him is
there peace; apart from Him there can be no future but one of
turmoil and tragedy.

The only effective peace agreement is the one written in
Christ's blood. It cleanses us of all the strife that consumes us
in our struggles with God and one another. Paul wrote to the
Ephesians, "For Christ himself has made peace ... by making
us all one people. He has broken down the wall of hostility that
used to separate us" (Ephesians 2:14). Only godly individuals
and nations, of course, will know the kind of peace Paul is
describing. We are the soldiers who mobilize to spread the
wonderful gospel of Christ's liberation all over the world. We
are the soldiers who fight in the knowledge that our victory is
already secure.

Peace is a wonderful ministry of the Holy Spirit, who knits

believers tightly together. Only the Holy Spirit can banish the barriers dividing the human race—nationality, race, econom-

ics, politics, age, gender—and mold our hearts together. If the Spirit is truly guiding us, we cannot help seeing that such barriers must come down: "There is one body and one Spirit—just as you were called to one hope when you were called—one Lord, one faith, one baptism; one God and Father of all, who is over all and through all and in all" (Ephesians 4:4–6 NIV).

We are not called to divisions or differentiations among believers, but to one Spirit, one Lord, one faith, and one baptism. Our God deeply desires us to experience the unity of being one body—the body of Christ. Too many of our churches, as I am certain you have observed, dissipate their energy in all kinds of divisions based on worldly standards such as wealth, age, race, music preferences, or insignificant doctrinal squabbles. The Spirit calls us not to divide ourselves but to combine our love and our gifts toward unity with all true believers.

ONE HOLY SPIRIT

We are not only one body, but one Spirit. The Holy Spirit in our lives creates a wonderful unity that surpasses all man-made boundaries. A friend who has ministered for many years to Christians in the People's Republic of China believes that the Communist government is fearful of Christians. Why? Because of their unity. Through the power of one Spirit, believers transcend political boundaries. They are believers first and Chinese second, a fact he believes the government finds frightening.

When we realize that there is but one Holy Spirit among us, we begin to see the foolishness of getting caught up in quarrels. Is the Spirit within you different from the Spirit within your fellow believers? That Spirit would never encourage a fracture of any kind within Christ's fellowship. He seeks to knit you together in love. If you or your Christian friends or your church become bogged down in conflict, perhaps you need to discover whether you are in step with God's Spirit.

Is the Spirit within you different from the Spirit within your fellow believers?

ONE HOPE, ONE LORD

We also have unity in the manner of our hope. We share one hope because we share one Lord. We are diverse, no matter how strong our unity. We come in many nationalities, and we worship in many styles. But the Lord our God is one God. As I have traveled throughout the world over the past fifty years, I have observed that the moment I am with other believers, we know we are brothers and sisters because of our mutual love for our Lord. Our clothing, our culture, our language, and our customs may differ, but the Lord who binds us together is one and the same. He does not change.

Paul explains this glorious truth: "But we know that there is only one God, the Father, who created everything, and we exist for him. And there is only one Lord, Jesus Christ, through whom God made everything and through whom we have been given life" (1 Corinthians 8:6).

ONE FAITH

Another attribute we have in common is one faith. This is a point that must be explained rather carefully. As we all know, there are many theological differences among believers. For example, there are many points of contention about the smaller matters of practice in worship. Doctrinal controversies and disagreements are all around us. So how is it that we say we have one faith? It is true because the Spirit is the One who shapes our faith. We may make many mistakes and take many wrong turns, which leads to disunity. But the genuine faith that is molded by the Holy Spirit will lead us together in unity and agreement if we will only follow Him.

There is one faith, though many misapplications of it. The Holy Spirit will always guide truly surrendered believers to the essentials. He will convict us of the reality of one crucified, resurrected, and living Christ who will return. He will lead us to trust His Word and to devote ourselves to prayer. These are givens, and any variation from them is a sign of the Spirit's absence. There is one faith as promoted by the Spirit, and that faith can only unify us because it is the same for all of us.

GETTING ALONG IN GOD'S FAMILY

As believers, we are all one body. We share one Spirit, one hope, one Lord, and one faith. We share the same glorious heavenly Father, for we have been adopted into His spiritual family. All of these biblical truths point to our unity as believers.

But we know that many believers do not experience the unity of the body of Christ. To walk together in unity requires drawing closer and closer to our brothers and sisters in the

Spirit's power. In fact, this can be seen as a strong leading indicator of spiritual health. If we find that strong and supportive Christian fellowship is missing from our lives, it is a good indication that we do not know the practical meaning of Holy Spirit unity. We can remedy this problem by taking a close look at the character qualities He is constantly developing within us.

As the Spirit molds us closer to Christ's image, we will grow in the humility of Christ. It certainly does not come naturally to this selfish and prideful world. Sin grows from pride, but humility maintains a proper and accurate perception of who we

While pride creates division, humility enhances unity.

are in God's great scheme of things. Humility prompts us to pour ourselves out for others, just as Christ poured himself out for us. While pride creates division, humility enhances unity.

We must be gentle. We must be patient. Above all, love is absolutely essential to unity among us. True love, the kind discussed in 1 Corinthians 13, is available only through the Holy Spirit. This is why, throughout my years of ministry, I have so frequently spoken and written on the subject of how to love others *by faith* through the enabling of the Holy Spirit. We could never achieve supernatural, sacrificial love without allowing Him to love us and to love others through us. When we invite God to love people through us, miracles can and will happen.

COOPERATING WITH THE PEACEMAKER

Building unity is only part of what is required. We must also strive to maintain the harmony we have sacrificed to attain. I can assure you that our adversary, the Devil, will use all of his schemes to break up our fellowship, for he knows that

Christians become truly dangerous when they come together to form the body of Christ.

The acrostic "UNITY" will help you remember some ways you can cooperate with the Holy Spirit to protect unity.

*U*nderstand the Perspectives of Others

Is it not amazing how differently we see the world when we stop to take a second look from the other person's perspective?

A little humility should help us "keep the main thing the main thing." In the New Testament, the unity of believers is a main emphasis. In disputes over minor matters of faith, we tend to put all our focus on who is in the right and who is in the wrong. The precise answer may typically be less important than we think. From the Spirit's perspective, what is *always* vitally important is how well we love and support each other.

*N*urture a Spirit of Forgiveness, not Bitterness

The world is filled with people who desperately need to be forgiven—and even more who need to forgive. Bitterness is that terrible weed that springs up in the soul and eventually chokes out all that is pure within us. It obscures our vision and perspective. It dominates our thoughts. It becomes a looming obstacle that cuts us off from perfect fellowship with God. Bitterness often begins over the smallest, most trivial slight—maybe even an imagined one. If unchecked, the root of bitterness will grow by feeding upon itself.

Jesus taught us to pray, "Forgive us our sins—just as we forgive those who have sinned against us" (Luke 11:4). The Holy Spirit wants to give us the power for that kind of forgiveness.

Initiate the Building of Bridges between Factions

I think we can all agree that there are enough walls in this world. Why is it that we find it impossible to work out our differences, all the while claiming to be guided by the Holy Spirit who craves unity and reconciliation? We need to knock down walls and build bridges in their place.

> *We need to knock down walls and build bridges in their place.*

Is your life more distinguished by bridges of love and harmony or by barriers of conflict and discord? How can you make peace among those torn by strife? Ask the Holy Spirit to guide you.

Treat Others with Love

God's will is clear: "Most important of all, continue to show deep love for each other, for love covers a multitude of sins" (1 Peter 4:8).

Jesus said, "If you are kind only to your friends, how are you different from anyone else? Even pagans do that" (Matthew 5:47). Here is the ultimate test of your love for others. What is it that separates you from any nonbeliever? Those who are able to love their enemies give evidence of a supernatural force at work in their lives. Love will turn an enemy into a brother.

Can we practice love in daily life? Let God show love through you, in unity and harmony, and the world will come hurrying to learn more about the One who inspires such love and unity.

*Y*ield to One Another out of Respect for Christ

Most of us can love in principle; the hard part is loving by application.

If we can love one another, we can yield to one another. Yielding is the outward proof of inner love. If you truly love your fellow believers, you will submit to them frequently for the good of the body and the will of the Lord. There can be healthy and positive discussion of alternatives, but love requires us to yield frequently. The Spirit will gently prod you on those occasions when you need to step back and put aside your pride.

> *"Your love for one another will prove to the world that you are my disciples."*
> —*Jesus Christ*

Jesus said, "Your love for one another will prove to the world that you are my disciples" (John 13:35). The Spirit's love and unity are miraculous, unique, and beyond anything the world can possibly manufacture.

Ask the Holy Spirit today to make you an instrument of His divine love to promote unity in your family, church, community, and country.

11

Your Protector from Evil

I t happens all around us: an invisible war. You are a fighter
in it, and I am, too. This war is the conflict that we as
Christians call spiritual warfare.

Make no mistake: This is authentic war with authentic,
invisible enemies. The Word of God tells us, "For we are
not fighting against people made of flesh and blood, but
against the evil rulers and authorities of the unseen world,
against those mighty powers of darkness who rule this
world, and against wicked spirits in the heavenly realms"
(Ephesians 6:12).

Satan entices the mind, titillates the senses, and uses our
areas of weakness to provoke sin and ruin the purity of our fellowship. It is no wonder that Jesus taught His disciples to pray,
"Don't let us yield to temptation, but deliver us from the evil
one" (Matthew 6:13).

But if the Enemy is a powerful creature rather than one of
flesh and blood, and if he is infinitely more intelligent than we
are, and if he has had all of human history to perfect his deceit
and trickery, how can we possibly hope to do battle with him—

let alone win? Surely, friends, we cannot, and we are foolish to try. But God can, and through His Holy Spirit, who indwells us, He does.

The Bible reveals that we have spiritual weaponry for fighting spiritual battles: "Put on all of God's armor so that you will be able to stand firm against all strategies and tricks of the Devil" (Ephesians 6:11). Paul made use of the Roman military terminology of his day to help us understand that indeed, life is a spiritual battle; we cannot afford to go out unprepared.

> *The Bible reveals that we have spiritual weaponry for fighting spiritual battles.*

Faith, salvation, truth, the Word—we seldom think of these as armor, but this is precisely what they are. If believers are going to stop surrendering to the flesh, the world, and the Devil, we must learn to fight spiritually. We must put on all the armor of the spiritual warrior.

For many centuries, Christian scholars have spoken of a three-pronged attack that believers must face when encountering temptation: the world, the flesh, and the Devil. They are interrelated, and they overlap—but you should consider each individually in order to better comprehend how the Holy Spirit serves as your protector from evil.

TEMPTATIONS OF THE WORLD

In the Bible, "the world" is a term that refers to the ordered, arranged system of physical reality that is under Satan's control. The Devil is referred to as "the prince of this world" (John 12:31). Biblically speaking, the world includes those who follow his deceptions as well as their false beliefs. We are "worldly," then, when we get out of step with the guiding Holy

Spirit and fall in line with Satan's crooked way—when we come under the influences of worldly people, values, or convictions.

Worldliness can be very subtle. Many Christians fall under the spell of material-ism, for example. But there

Worldliness can be very subtle.

are many other forms of worldliness. To combat the lure of this world, we should reflect on the following Scripture:

> Stop loving this evil world and all that it offers you, for
> when you love the world, you show that you do not have
> the love of the Father in you. For the world offers only the
> lust for physical pleasure, the lust for everything we see,
> and pride in our possessions. These are not from the
> Father. They are from this evil world. And this world is
> fading away, along with everything it craves. But if you do
> the will of God, you will live forever.
>
> 1 JOHN 2:15–17

TEMPTATIONS OF THE FLESH

The biblical term "flesh" refers to the earthly part of mankind, or lusts and desires that are contrary to God's perfect design for us. His Word teaches that living according to the flesh is a sure road to death. The way of the flesh includes not only lust, gluttony, and other inappropriate appetites, but also destructive impulses such as anger and greed. When we ignore the guidance of the Spirit, we are certain to live in the flesh and will make ourselves as shallow and miserable as the rest of the world.

Praise God that His Spirit helps us crucify the flesh! If you are a slave to impulsive eating, the Spirit will help you place that fleshly sin on the cross, where Christ has already died to keep it from having power over you. If you struggle to control your thoughts from sexual impurity, the Spirit will help you put that tendency to death. Much of our spiritual growth and maturity comes through the painful sacrifice of cooperating with the Spirit, moment by moment and day by day.

❖

Our old sinful selves were crucified with Christ so that sin might lose its power in our lives. (Romans 6:6)

Here's a biblical promise to remember: "Our old sinful selves were crucified with Christ so that sin might lose its power in our lives. We are no longer slaves to sin.... So you should consider yourselves dead to sin and able to live for the glory of God through Christ Jesus" (Romans 6:6–11).

TEMPTATIONS OF THE DEVIL

The third attack of sin and temptation is that of the Devil himself. He is ultimately behind all temptation; he is the unseen enemy. But there are times when he steps forward to challenge us personally. This is why the Bible admonishes us, "Be careful! Watch out for attacks from the Devil, your great enemy. He prowls around like a roaring lion, looking for some victim to devour" (1 Peter 5:8).

But what will happen when we stand tall against Satan? How astonished will the world be to see us stand firm under the attack of the worst temptations he has to offer? You cannot face the lion from hell unless you have the strength of the Lion of Judah. He will protect you through spiritual warfare with the armor of God. He will shelter you with the shield of faith and help you strike back using the sword of the Spirit, the Word of God. We can triumph over Satan in the coliseum of life because the Victor himself, Jesus Christ, lives within us through His Spirit.

WINNING AGAINST TEMPTATION

Claiming the admonitions and promises of God's Word, and in the power of the Spirit, you can indeed win over temptation! Here are several practical ways you can cooperate with the Holy Spirit in standing strong against the ways of the world, the flesh, and the Devil.

CLAIM GOD'S PROMISES FOR VICTORY

The Scriptures offer us powerful ammunition for standing firm in the times we are most tempted. Note several liberating promises in the following passage alone:

> No temptation has overtaken you but such as is common to
> man; and God is faithful, who will not allow you to be
> tempted beyond what you are able, but with the tempta-
> tion will provide the way of escape also, that you will be
> able to endure it.
>
> 1 CORINTHIANS 10:13 NASB

When we struggle on the verge of disobedience, we feel isolated and alone. We think that no one can help, that no one can understand what we are experiencing. But the Bible promises that other people also face such temptations every day and that God never fails to provide self-control to His children when they seek His help.

God never fails to provide self-control to His children when they seek His help.

Not only that, but the temptation will never be sizeable enough that we cannot win over it. God does not allow a temptation so big that you cannot overcome it with His help! He always offers an escape route.

OCCUPY YOUR MIND WITH THOUGHTS THAT PLEASE GOD

The Bible urges us, "Don't copy the behavior and customs of this world, but let God transform you into a new person by changing the way you think. Then you will know what God wants you to do, and you will know how good and pleasing and perfect his will really is" (Romans 12:2).

UNITE WITH OTHER BELIEVERS IN WARFARE PRAYER

"The earnest prayer of a righteous person has great power and wonderful results" (James 5:16). God will honor you for your humility in seeking the prayerful support of your fellow Christians. He will bless not only your life but the lives of those who come to your aid. It is also true that you will be far less likely to commit a sin when your friends and family are holding you accountable.

RESIST SATAN AND HIS SCHEMES

If we allow the Holy Spirit and His power to reside in us, Satan cannot crush us. The Holy Spirit is always capable of resisting Satan and his schemes.

The apostle James urges us, "Submit yourselves, then, to God. Resist the devil, and he will flee from you. Come near to God and he will come near to you" (James 4:7–8 NIV). We can be victorious in our struggle against Satan, but in order to do so we must (1) submit our will to God, (2) resist Satan, and (3) draw near to God.

As we daily give our bodies, our lives, and our all to our

wonderful Creator God and Savior, He empowers us to resist Satan. And as we resist Satan in the power of the Holy Spirit, we are promised that he will flee from us.

God uses Satan to test our faithfulness and develop our character. But He lets Satan go only so far. There is always a leash, if you will, on Satan and what he is allowed to do in the life of a believer. However, through our willful disobedience, we can give

> *You will be far less likely to commit a sin when your friends and family are holding you accountable.*

Satan access to us by stepping out from behind God's hedge of protection and into Satan's range of attack. Perhaps this is why the apostle Paul admonished, "When angry, do not sin; do not ever let your wrath (your exasperation, your fury or indignation) last until the sun goes down. Leave no [such] room or foothold for the devil [give no opportunity to him]" (Ephesians 4:26–27 AB).

Any unresolved sin gives Satan an opening to attack us. By refusing to confess and repent from our sin, over time we enable Satan to establish even more of a beachhead within us. From there he can launch more attacks and gain even more access to our life. When we tolerate sin in our life, we provide Satan with an access point through the hedge of protection God has placed around us. We provide the Enemy with the very resources he can use to injure us. And injure us he will!

For this reason, it is extremely dangerous to treat sin lightly. It is the poison our Enemy uses for our destruction. But God will protect those who remain faithful. The psalmist promised, "The angel of the LORD encamps around those who fear him, and he delivers them" (Psalm 34:7 NIV).

ARM YOURSELF WITH THE SWORD OF THE SPIRIT

The apostle Paul rightly referred to the Holy Scriptures as the "sword of the Spirit." When you equip yourself with the Word of God by studying and applying its guidance and promises, you will find that it accomplishes what nothing else can. Consider what the writer of Hebrews observed:

> For the word of God is full of living power. It is sharper than the sharpest knife, cutting deep into our innermost thoughts and desires. It exposes us for what we really are. Nothing in all creation can hide from him. Everything is naked and exposed before his eyes. This is the God to whom we must explain all that we have done.
>
> HEBREWS 4:12–13

The Scriptures literally have the power to penetrate to the deepest level of a person. They have the ability to do corrective surgery in your soul, your spirit, and your mind. They can cleanse your heart, bring about change, and cut away Satan's grip on you.

What is your most troublesome temptation? Whatever it might be, I have confidence that you can stand firm against it. But never attempt to do so without the proper weapon in your hand. You should always arm yourself with the sword of the Spirit. Our greatest weapon in the face of inner conflict is the Word of God wielded with the power of the Spirit of God.

God's Word is the objective, eternal truth for all believers. God's Spirit, on the other hand, is His presence in our individual lives. If we had the Bible alone, the truth would seem cold and impersonal; if we had only the Holy Spirit, the truth might be subjectively misapplied based on our personal biases. But when we put the objective Word in the hands of the Spirit who knows us individually and intimately, there is no crisis we cannot face. There is no temptation too big to overcome!

CHOOSE WISELY!

Jesus taught that we cannot love the world and love God too. "No one can serve two masters. For you will hate one and love the other, or be devoted to one and despise the other. You cannot serve both God and money" (Matthew 6:24).

We must make a choice—sometimes many, many times a day—between yielding to the world's way, our fleshly desires, or Satan himself ... or to the Holy Spirit. The key to guarding our affections is abiding in the Holy Spirit.

EXPECT GOD TO PREVAIL

The British have a term for the way in which a nineteenth-century military officer was to face opposition. It is the word "steady." When faced with a horde of enemy soldiers wielding swords and thundering toward him on horseback, the commander was to remember his past experiences in battle. Then he was to review his regiment's capabilities. Finally, now confident of victory, he was to contemplate the sense of accomplishment a successfully conducted battle would give him. And so in the face of overwhelming opposition, a British officer remained "steady."

We, too, can remain "steady." In the presence of sustained and overwhelming opposition, we need to remember the Lord's past accomplishments in our lives, His current efforts, and His assurance of ultimate victory.

Remember the biblical promise: "In all these things we are more than conquerors through him who loved us" (Romans 8:37 NIV).

12

Your Source for Service

L ike all great art, you bear the stamp and style of the artist who produced you. God created you as a thing of beauty to last for all eternity. Best of all, you are an active work of art. You are a masterpiece created with a function: to do "good things" that He laid out for you even before you were born.

Think of a loving human father who is waiting for his infant son to be born. He buys a baseball glove and places it in the closet, eager for his child to reach the age when he can discover the joy of breaking in that glove and playing catch with Dad. The father dreams of that moment. This is the joy God feels about your spiritual gifts. This is how He awaits your discovery of the work He has set aside for you.

Even now, you are a masterpiece whether you realize it or not. But the best is yet to come! When you discover what the Father created you to do and you begin to fulfill that bright destiny, your joy will be exceeded only by the joy of your Creator, who planned it all along. In this chapter we will talk about those thrilling tasks and gifts that await you.

GOD GAVE YOU SPECIAL "GIFTS"

Have you ever thought about how God sees your life? He sees past, present, and future as if they were all one, for He does not dwell within time as we do. Our minutes, days, and years are a created structure within His eternity. From His place in eternity, He looks upon your life as a whole unit. He knows the gifts He designed for you, and He knows the tasks that need to be fulfilled. He carefully crafted your gifts and your personality to fill those needs, and He placed you in just the right position to be confronted by those needs one day. All that remains is for you to discover the gifts, find the need, and do what God designed you to do.

On the day the Holy Spirit entered your life at salvation, those gifts began to percolate, even if you were unaware of them. The Spirit is the One who activates those gifts and begins to mold them toward service. He is the one who lightly nudges you and whispers in your ear when you come to the moment of exercising them—like the young son taking out that baseball glove for the first time.

It is also the Spirit who works powerfully through your gifts, in ways that will astound you. "Aha!" you will gasp. "This is the very thing I was meant to do. In this, I can fulfill my potential for God, and it feels good." You will have discovered something precious and irreplaceable: dynamic purpose for your life. God has a wonderful plan for your life, and you have taken the first steps toward discovering what it is. Trust Him, and He will lead you every step of the way along the exciting journey.

GIFTS ARE FOR GIVING

One of the most wonderful traits of spiritual gifts is the way they bond you with other believers. God gives them to you for edifying others. Unless you use your gifts, something will be missing in your local Christian fellowship. People will lack something of value. And if others fail to use their gifts, you will lack something as well.

It is no coincidence that the Bible calls the church the "body of Christ." He is the head, and each of us is a body part. "Just as our bodies have many parts and each part has a special function, so it is with Christ's body. We are all parts of his one body, and each of us has different work to do. And since we are all one body in Christ, we belong to each other, and each of us needs all the others" (Romans 12:4–5). Jesus left the world forty days after His resurrection, but in a miraculous manner He created a way to continue being present and active in it. His body lives and walks and serves through the accumulation of believers, indwelt by the Spirit, who are using their spiritual gifts for His purposes.

Our Lord created His church to be a community that works with the same beautiful complexity as the parts of a human body. The human body is God's physical masterpiece, and the church is His spiritual one. In both cases, a wound to one part means pain for the whole body. A broken finger means that a physical body will feel the ache and be hampered in all that it tries to do. A suffering church member means that the body of Christ will experience pain and malfunction. We were never intended to be independent agents as believers. We need each other vitally, and we cannot fully experience the Christian life without the give and take of functioning in the body.

It is a great mistake to suppose that all Christians should be carbon copies of one another, for diversity is what allows us to accomplish such a wide array of tasks in building God's kingdom. Instead of allowing our differences to divide us, we should realize that they are the very distinctions that make us special. Diversity shows the genius of God's design. He made us with unique gifts, varying perspectives, and distinct personalities so we can work together as a healthy body and complete the tasks He has for us.

You are a vital part of the body of Christ!

The glue that holds the body of Christ together, of course, is the Holy Spirit. Without the Spirit we would have no hope of ever finding unity. It is the same Spirit who allows one to be a helper and another a teacher, one to be an administrator and another an encourager. When we are in tune with Him, we see the big picture; we recognize the marvelous ways in which we complement one another. God has a vital purpose for you, and His Spirit will enable you to fulfill whatever He needs you to do.

As we dwell on this remarkable truth, it is important to pause a moment and remember that in no way should a spiritual gift puff us up with pride or fill us with any delusions of grandeur. Should we ever attempt to flaunt a spiritual gift or exercise it in ways that belie humility or do not glorify God, it will be corrupted into a destructive, divisive distraction. (Unfortunately, many of us have seen this happen.) Beware the temptation to take pride in a spiritual gift. True gifts of the Spirit never point to our glory, but only to the magnificence of Christ.

PUTTING YOUR GIFTS TO WORK

Two thousand years ago, Jesus lived upon the earth and ministered to people. After He departed for heaven to sit at the right hand of the Father, He appointed His Spirit to carry on His work through us—not in a vague, symbolic sense but in a true, supernatural one.

- Jesus once delivered His teachings in Israel; He now delivers them across the world through us.

- He once traveled among all the towns and provinces there; He now travels to every inhabited continent and nation through us.

- He once performed miracles to the people of His time; He now performs them in our time through us.

- He once healed people, loved people, encouraged people, and showed them a new way to live. All of those things are happening today through you and me as we manifest our gifts as His living body.

We are His hands, His feet, and His presence in the world. And it's all to glorify Him.

God wants His children to experience the contentment and joy that come from serving Him in the power of the Holy Spirit. Here are several practical ways you can bring honor to Him through the use of your spiritual gifts:

LET LOVE BE YOUR MOTIVATOR

Never let your focus drift to yourself; keep it on serving Christ and His body. As always, the key to doing that is found in the most wonderful of all words: *love.* No matter what you accomplish, no matter how hard you work, your gifts will amount to nothing without love. (See 1 Corinthians 13.)

If you begin to regard others as more important than yourself and look to their well-being, you will find yourself using your gifts in love—almost without realizing it. Used in the service of love for Christ and His church, your spiritual gifts will make an eternal impact.

IDENTIFY YOUR GIFTS

Some ministries have developed simple written tests to help you think about your aptitudes and tendencies, and thus discover what your gifts might be. But the best way for you to learn what the Spirit has equipped you to do is through service. Minister in a wide variety of opportunities and discover where you are most effective, where you derive the greatest satisfaction, where Christ is most glorified, and where your fellow believers are most strengthened. I believe that if you set about doing this in your church, you will soon begin to learn to identify your spiritual gifts.

DEVELOP YOUR GIFTS

The apostle Paul wrote to Timothy, "Fan into flames the spiritual gift God gave you when I laid my hands on you" (2 Timothy 1:6).

Three components play a part in developing your spiritual gifts: (1) the empowering of the Holy Spirit, (2) dedicated work on your part, and (3) an appreciable amount of time over which the work of the Holy Spirit, coupled with your efforts, bring about maturity in your life. Be patient and diligent. No matter what your spiritual gift, use it and nurture it and see what results the Lord has in store!

REMEMBER: YOU ARE ONE PART OF THE BODY

The apostle Paul wrote to the Christians in Rome, "As God's messenger, I give each of you this warning: Be honest in your estimate of yourselves, measuring your value by how much faith God has given you" (Romans 12:3).

If we happen to be given some of the more visible spiritual

gifts, such as preaching and teaching, we should not feel more important than others. And if we have less visible gifts, such as helping and mercy, we should not feel less important. All the gifts are necessary for the health of the body of Christ. And all the gifts are a result of God's grace to us. We did not earn them and we never will. We must give all the glory to God.

Whatever your spiritual gift, I encourage you to serve humbly and gratefully, always remembering that we are useless apart from our brothers and sisters in Christ, the power of the Holy Spirit, and our glorious Lord and Savior, Jesus Christ.

SERVE OTHERS HUMBLY AND JOYFULLY

The Bible declares, "For you have been called to live in freedom—not freedom to satisfy your sinful nature, but freedom to serve one another in love" (Galatians 5:13).

Jesus Christ, God's Son, is our ultimate example of service. We may sometimes feel too important or too busy to serve, but Jesus was God, King of the universe! No one was more important or had more reason to be "too busy." Yet, because of His great love for us He humbled himself, washed His disciples' feet, and even died for our sin. As He stated, "For even I, the Son of Man, came here not to be served but to serve others, and to give my life as a ransom for many" (Matthew 20:28).

I can assure you that serving in the power of the Holy Spirit will bring you the greatest fulfillment life has to offer.

DON'T BE THE MISSING PIECE

You are one piece of a great, worldwide jigsaw puzzle whose picture of the eternal body of Christ has yet to be completely assembled. There can be nothing more forlorn and useless than a puzzle piece that has fallen to the floor, been swept under the carpet, and languishes apart from the rest of the puzzle. Without that one piece, the big picture can never be complete. The piece itself has no value. But when it is found, and when it settles into the puzzle with a satisfying click, all of the puzzle's shapes and colors suddenly fit with perfect precision. The puzzle piece interlocks properly on every side and helps to make a beautiful picture.

The use of gifts under the Spirit's direction is the missing piece to the puzzle of modern Christianity. The Bible admonishes this:

God has given each of us the ability to do certain things well. So if God has given you the ability to prophesy, speak out when you have faith that God is speaking through you. If your gift is that of serving others, serve them well. If you are a teacher, do a good job of teaching. If your gift is to encourage others, do it! If you have money, share it generously. If God has given you leadership ability, take the responsibility seriously. And if you have a gift for showing kindness to others, do it gladly.

ROMANS 12:6–8

Too many of our congregations are struggling to justify their existence and protect their slumping attendance, and much of that is because believers are not putting their gifts to work. The church is not ministering to needs as it should. We can and must do better, and it can begin with you. Find and exercise your spiritual gifts, and help all your fellow believers do the same.

13

Your Empowerment for Evangelism

I f we are truthful, we must admit that we are sometimes indifferent about the souls of certain people.

There is the man who cuts us off in traffic. The uncaring receptionist at the other end of a telephone line. The slow, tiresome person ahead of us in line at the grocery store. We even have friends with whom we never attempt to discuss the most important news the world has ever heard—the good news of Jesus Christ.

We know we should share the wonderful, life-changing news of the gospel, but we are afraid. We feel inadequate, or we think other things are more important. Perhaps most of all, though we wouldn't want to admit it, we lack the love that would compel us to tell others about Jesus.

Meanwhile, God loves every single one of these lost, lonely people with an everlasting love. He desperately yearns to reach them. But He yearns to reach them *through us.* God's way is to rescue people through other people. He has sprinkled us around the world to be "the salt of the earth" (Matthew 5:13), a preservative against immorality. He has set us ablaze with His glory to be the "light of the world" (Matthew 5:14), illuminating the path to Jesus for others.

How important is it that we share our faith? It was so important to Jesus that His final words to His disciples before He ascended to heaven were, "Go into all the world and preach the Good News to everyone, everywhere" (Mark 16:15). By making these His last words, Jesus underscored the priority He places on sharing the good news with others. These are our marching orders—job one for this lifetime.

Many Christians believe that evangelism is one small part of our faith, or that it is a particular gift for those who are called to it. But we know two things from the Great Commission: Bearing witness to our faith, or "witnessing" as many Christians refer to it, is at the very heart of Christianity. Paul wrote to the Corinthians, "We are Christ's ambassadors, and God is using us to speak to you. We urge you, as though Christ himself were here pleading with you, 'Be reconciled to God!'" (2 Corinthians 5:20). Therefore, we should share our faith as full-time ambassadors, and with the love of Christ himself speaking through us.

But it is not we who do it, but the Holy Spirit who does it through us. He longs to do it through you, and guess what? He knows how! Let Him do it!

NOT IN OUR OWN POWER

Jesus said, "When the Holy Spirit has come upon you, you will receive power and will tell people about me everywhere—in Jerusalem, throughout Judea, in Samaria, and to the ends of the earth" (Acts 1:8). We cannot fail to notice that in both Matthew 28:19–20 and Acts 1:8, Jesus emphasizes the empowerment of the Spirit for our witnessing. I believe that if more Christians realized the implications of this truth, there would be much less fear and hesitation over telling others about Jesus.

If the Spirit did not speak through you, you would have little success leading others to Christ. But because He promises to be with you "always, even to the end of the age," you can be confident of your ability to share your faith successfully.

Add this promise from Jesus to His disciples: "Now I will send the Holy Spirit, just as my Father promised. But stay here in the city until the Holy Spirit comes and fills you with power from heaven" (Luke 24:49). Is it not interesting that pending the arrival of the Spirit, Jesus actually restrained His disciples from going out into the world and talking about Him? Without the Spirit's enabling, all our efforts would be in vain; with Him, we can turn the world upside down.

GENTLE PERSUASION

There is a great misconception about evangelism: Many people believe it has something to do with winning an argument. Naturally, arguing is the worst way to convince someone of anything. Pride becomes involved, two sides square off, and it is unlikely that anyone will leave with a changed mind. Certainly when it comes to witnessing, we need not argue or contend with people intellectually. No one is ever debated into the kingdom of God. It is our role to practice gentle persuasion, and it is the Holy Spirit who

> *No one is ever debated into the kingdom of God.*

does the persuading. He works in the hearts and minds of the people to whom we witness. He bursts through mental barriers to convict people of the truth.

The real issue with nonbelievers is usually not an intellectual one; it is an issue of the will. It is the role of the Holy Spirit to break down those barriers and provide the answers. We can be certain that the Spirit will remove an individual's barriers of doubt. But He does something else as well: He convicts people of their sin and their need for salvation.

We often worry about how we can persuade a nonbeliever to be saved from his sin when he refuses to acknowledge the existence of sin. Again, we simply need to take God at His Word that the Spirit will accomplish His work, in His own time, in the hearts and minds of those to whom we witness. God proclaimed through the prophet Isaiah, "It is the same with my word. I send it out, and it always produces fruit. It will accomplish all I want it to, and it will prosper everywhere I send it" (Isaiah 55:11).

In short, God is sovereign. If He desires to reach out to someone with the gospel through you or me, He will do so. It is our responsibility to obey and share God's love and plan of salvation.

But how will we know what to say?

EMPOWERED BY THE SPIRIT

If the Spirit can work within the mind of the friend to whom you are witnessing, He can work inside you, too. When salvation is on the line, be certain that the Spirit will provide you with the right words to say to your friend.

The Spirit will speak through you, and He will use Scripture as His sword to penetrate a person's soul and spirit. I hope you will always have your Bible with you when you share your faith, even if it is a small New Testament that fits in your pocket. Take some time to learn the key verses that underscore God's love for everyone; mankind's sinful nature and our need for salvation; God's provision of His Son, Jesus Christ, to pay the price for our sin; and how one can accept Christ in his or her life as Savior and Lord.

> God's love—John 3:16
>
> God's plan—John 17:3
>
> Man is sinful—Romans 3:23
>
> Man is separated—Romans 6:23
>
> Jesus died in our place—Romans 5:8
>
> Jesus rose from the dead—1 Corinthians 15:3–6
>
> Jesus is the only way to God—John 14:6
>
> We must receive Christ—John 1:12
>
> We receive Christ through faith—Ephesians 2:8–9
>
> When we receive Christ, we experience a new birth—John
> 3:1–8
>
> We receive Christ through personal invitation—Revelation
> 3:20
>
> The Bible promises eternal life to all who receive Christ—
> 1 John 5:11–12

Never worry in advance about whether your friend accepts the Bible as God's authoritative Word. This is irrelevant; what matters is that the Spirit accepts the Word and uses it powerfully. The truth will cut through with precision, as the writer of Hebrews reminds us: "The word of God is full of living power. It is sharper than the sharpest knife, cutting deep into our innermost thoughts and desires. It exposes us for what we really are" (Hebrews 4:12).

Many years ago, as I contemplated an easy-to-understand way to present the gospel, I thought of how scientists had discovered certain natural "laws" of our universe, such as the law of gravity and the law of thermodynamics. It occurred to me that God had also designed His creation with certain "spiritual laws" as presented to us in His Word. Four in particular stood out to me; together, they formed a concise, yet essentially complete, overview of God's wonderful plan for our salvation.

I wrote out these four principles and the Scripture verses from which they came, and titled the presentation *The Four Spiritual Laws*. Over the decades, the Spirit has used this simple gospel presentation to help millions of believers lead others to Christ. If you feel inadequately prepared to share your faith with others, let me suggest that you consider using a presentation such as this as a starting place in your witnessing opportunities. Book 10 of "The Joy of Knowing God" series, *The Joy of Sharing Jesus,* provides an overview of *The Four Spiritual Laws* along with some proven coaching to help you present the gospel effectively using this simple method.

There is no magic in the method, I assure you. In our ministry, we do not claim that *The Four Spiritual Laws* is necessarily the best method, nor is it the only method, to share Christ with others. It is simply an easy-to-use-and-understand distillation of the gospel message, presented in a simple, logical manner. Any success we have experienced through *The Four Spiritual Laws* is not of us, but totally of God's Spirit at work in the hearts of the men, women, and young people who have yielded their hearts and lives to Christ through the power of God's Word.

In fact, I have often said this. Those words invariably cause a few raised eyebrows, which settle back down when my listeners realize that these words are literally true: It is not me but the Holy Spirit who does the leading—all of it—and it is He who has given me the privilege of praying with many of people as they received Christ. No one can experience salvation unless it is through the work of the Holy Spirit.

SUCCESSFUL WITNESSING IS ...

What a relief to know that it is the Holy Spirit, not us, who is responsible for producing fruit! Our role is simply to heed His prompting whenever opportunities become available to tell others the good news. Perhaps the following definition of successful witnessing will help liberate you from thinking that "convincing and converting souls" is up to you, as it has helped the hundreds of thousands of Christians we have had the privilege to train around the world:

Successful witnessing is simply taking the initiative to share Christ in the power of the Holy Spirit and leaving the results to God.

In addition, I have found the following guidelines helpful in telling others about Jesus Christ.

PRAY OFTEN FOR THOSE WHO DON'T KNOW JESUS

Too many Christians live out a lukewarm faith today, often because they are not sharing their faith in Christ with others. If they are not sharing their faith, it is because they lack a true burden for nonbelievers. If they lack a burden for the lost, it is because they lack the love that would result in such a burden. And if they lack that love, surely it is because they have not been praying daily for these people.

Do you remember to pray for the salvation of your loved ones, neighbors, and friends? If you have lacked the will to go and lovingly share Christ with these people, is it because you lack the will to pray for them? Bring their names before God daily and see if He does not give you the desire and the strength to talk with them about Christ's love and forgiveness.

TAKE THE INITIATIVE TO TALK ABOUT JESUS

When will that defining moment finally come about? It is up to you. With salvation and forgiveness so transforming and won-derful, life in Christ so abundant and joyful, fellowship with other believers so full and rewarding, why do we risk seeing someone die suddenly without hearing the incredible news of the one true way to heaven? If your friend were dying of can-cer and you had found the surefire cure, would you not share this cure with your friend with love and enthusiasm? Of course you would.

The conclusion is inescapable: We must obey the Spirit's prompts and take the initiative to share Christ at every opportunity.

NEVER ARGUE

God never desires for you to get caught up in words that divide—this is obviously the game of your adversary, the Devil. Remember to trust the Spirit, who is so much more powerful than Satan. Remember to love and to listen. Keep to God's Word, which will be empowered by the Spirit, and avoid argu-ments or tangential questions.

SHARE WHAT GOD HAS DONE FOR YOU

One thing no one can argue about is what God has done for you personally. I challenge you to prepare a personal three-minute testimony. Use the simple outline of what your life was like before you met Christ, how you received Christ, and what your life has been like since. Share the wonderful things He has done for you. You are living proof of the redemptive power of God, so be certain that your witness is warm and personal. Your listeners cannot help responding to the light that glows from your life and experience.

Speak Boldly, Stay on Track, Seek the Spirit's Guidance

If you keep these three simple words in mind—*speak* boldly, *stay* on track, and *seek* the Spirit's guidance—your witness will be compelling and fruitful. You speak boldly because you are an ambassador for Christ. You stay on track because, compared to what you have to say, any other subject would be trivial and inconsequential. And you seek the Spirit's guidance because with such a Guide there are no wrong turns to be taken, no poor words to be chosen, no lack of wisdom or discernment to possibly bring a shadow across your conversation.

Remember, it is your task to sow the seeds wherever possible. You cannot control where the seeds land, nor whether they take root. We are merely the sowers, you and I. The Spirit is the One who does the work in the hearts of those with whom we share. Let us sow abundantly—enabled by His power and trusting that His love and grace will do a miraculous work.

STEP BY STEP, GOD LAYS OUT HIS
SPECIAL PLAN FOR EACH OF US.

14

Your Counselor in Decision Making

Have you ever been faced with a difficult decision, one where there seemed to be no right or easy answer? Have you wished the solution was written neatly in the clouds or listed for quick reference in a book somewhere?

No one relishes making a significant decision when the important things in life are on the line.

Just the same, we all face those anxious moments. As Christians, we can rest in the assurance that we are never as isolated as we may feel at decision time. We have the Spirit to come alongside us, encourage us, empower us, and help us make the right decisions. "'For I know the plans I have for you,'" says the LORD. "'They are plans for good and not for disaster, to give you a future and a hope'" (Jeremiah 29:11).

Could any words be more reassuring? God knows the future already; it is not one of chance and chaos but one defined by His perfect plan, lovingly worked out with our welfare in mind. If we commit our plans to Him, no matter what we decide, He is with us and will steer us as we go. We need to learn to hear His gentle voice guiding us to do His work in this world, because that is exactly why we are here in the first place. Friend, let the Holy Spirit guide you from this moment forth, and rejoice that He will!

That does not mean we will always choose the right path in accordance with that perfect plan. We are fallen human beings, born again of the Spirit yet prey to the weakness of the flesh. We often choose impulsively. We decide without taking the Spirit's counsel or with an incorrect interpretation of it. The plan of God is perfect, but the steps of people are often faulty. Even the wisest of Christians have wandered from the right path at some time or another. So what should we do?

THE GOOD SHEPHERD DOES NOT MISLEAD

The solution, of course, is to learn to discern clearly the voice of the Master. Jesus compared himself to a good shepherd leading the flock. We must come to a humble realization that we are sheep who need a shepherd for every step. The landscape is full of deep pits and hungry wolves, and we need to be led toward the green pastures and quiet waters the Shepherd desires for us. We must know His voice and follow it obediently.

The Good Shepherd would never hide from His sheep nor lead them into a dangerous place.

Be assured that the Lord wants to lead you even more than you want to follow Him. The Good Shepherd would never hide from His sheep nor lead them into a dangerous place. God is eager for you to hear His voice, and you need only have the desire to heed it. Hearing God's voice is not only important for knowing the general plan that applies to all believers—abiding in prayer, studying the Word, living in purity, and so on—but also for knowing the personal plan that God has for each individual believer. For instance, as a Christian, you need not grapple with the question of whether to marry a nonbeliever; we know from the Word of God that being "unequally yoked" is forbidden. But you will need to confront the issue of whether to marry this Christian or that one, for this falls under the category of His personal plan for you.

COOPERATING WITH THE COUNSELOR

Step by step, God lays out His special plan for each of us. Rarely does He reveal everything all at once or as quickly as we may want to

Rarely does God reveal everything all at once or as quickly as we may want to know it.

know it. Perhaps this is because we would be terrified if we could see the entire picture from the very beginning. Or perhaps it is because He wants us to depend on Him every moment of every day. We may be interested in all the details of the plan, but He is more interested in the daily details of our relationship with Him. In our souls we may be saying, "Just tell me, Lord! I cannot wait—I want to know now!" But the gentle voice of the Spirit replies, "Be patient. Know Me well, and the future will take care of itself. We will work it out together, you and I, if you will simply trust Me." In His perfect time, God shows us what He wants us to see.

So how does the Spirit guide us toward the correct decision? The following guidelines provide the best counsel I can offer you in making godly decisions through the leadership of the Holy Spirit.

GROUND YOURSELF IN THE TRUTH OF GOD'S WORD

Let the Scriptures be the place where you go for refreshment, growth, and the sheer joy of knowing that God speaks to all generations through these words. As you dwell in the Scriptures, you will find that decision making becomes less of a chore. So many of our questions are already answered in this Book; so much of God's will is already spelled out for us.

Use your devotional time to listen to the Holy Spirit's leading. The most important part of our time with God is not what we say but what we hear and sense. Ask questions of the Lord and learn to discern His responses. Many believers keep a prayer journal, which can be an extremely rewarding and faith-building experience. Record answers to your requests and petitions as well as what God is teaching you and how He is personally leading you.

Young believers struggle in this area at times. They ask, "Why do I not hear God's voice? How will I know I am not imagining what He says?" Jesus told His disciples, "My sheep listen to my voice; I know them, and they follow me" (John 10:27 NIV). Little lambs may not know the shepherd's voice quite as well. They will stumble along and need a nudge from the sheep who are more mature. But God will not hide from you. Walk in the Spirit, totally surrendered to the One who created you, loves you, and died for you. Be patient, keep seeking, and you will learn to hear His voice.

SURRENDER YOUR WILL TO GOD CONTINUALLY

Why do we hesitate to lay all our desires before the One who desires nothing but good for us? It can only be a matter of trust. If we trust God's character, we will submit ourselves totally to His will. Submit yourself as Paul commends us to do:

> I plead with you to give your bodies to God. Let them be a living and holy sacrifice—the kind he will accept. When you think of what he has done for you, is this too much to ask? Don't copy the behavior and customs of this world, but let God transform you into a new person by changing the way you think. Then you will know what God wants you to do, and you will know how good and pleasing and perfect his will really is.
>
> ROMANS 12:1–2

ASK GOD FOR WISDOM AND DIRECTION

Do you believe that God wants you to stumble along in life, bereft of any guidance for doing the right thing? He would never entrust the building of His kingdom to such a system.

How many of your decisions, great and small, do you think the Holy Spirit wants to be involved in? The correct answer is all of them. He wants to partner with you in making your life as fruitful and fulfilling as possible. He never desires that you make a single wrong decision. I hope you will do as I try to do—stop in the midst of any crucial moment during the day and ask the Spirit to give you wisdom and direction. The Bible tells us we are to "pray without ceasing" (1 Thessalonians 5:17 NKJV). See how different your life will become when you begin depending upon His guidance throughout the day.

SEEK COUNSEL OF GODLY ADVISORS

Mature believers can serve as God's messengers to you. Often they will give you advice that might save you from months or years of disappointment and heartache. At the very least, it should give you pause when a trusted advisor counsels against the thing you are strongly considering. No matter how great your eagerness, you should stop and give the decision more time, simply because a wise person's advice is worth taking seriously. God can speak directly through our mentors and trusted friends. I would be very hesitant to fail to ask their advice or to ignore their words.

CONFESS ALL SIN TO GOD AND WALK IN OBEDIENCE

Too many people these days cringe at the word *obedience* while savoring the word *freedom*. But without obedience there can be no true freedom. Be obedient to God in the smallest details of your life, and thoroughly confess any sin that is revealed by the Spirit's conviction. Employ the metaphor of "Spiritual Breathing" we discussed earlier to confess and purify you throughout the day: "Exhale" by confessing your sins, then "inhale"—appropriate by faith the renewed fullness and empowerment of the Holy Spirit. This practice of Spiritual Breathing, if you are diligent about it, will keep you in fellowsip with God and better able to hear His voice as His Spirit guides you.

BELIEVE HIS PROMISE!

Our sovereign, omniscient Creator and Savior desires to guide us if we will only seek Him. Tune in every day to His frequency through prayer and reading God's Word. Believe His promise, "I will guide you along the best

pathway for your life. I will advise you and watch over you"
(Psalm 32:8).

A word of warning: As you follow the Holy Spirit's leading
and step out in faith, you may encounter opposition. This
opposition may come from the world, from your old sin nature,
or from Satan. Some believers think that when this happens,
either the Holy Spirit is not guiding them or God has closed a
door. They wonder how they can know the difference. But the
truth is that great blessings often follow great trials.

Every time you undertake a significant effort for the Lord,
you may experience difficult opposition. But if the Holy Spirit
is leading you, you will invariably triumph regardless of the
obstacles. God always blesses those who are obedient to Him,
who desire to do His will, and who daily walk in His Holy
Spirit. "We can make our plans, but the LORD determines our
steps" (Proverbs 16:9). Ask God to teach you to lean on the
Spirit's guidance for every decision you make!

WALK IN THE SPIRIT, KEEP IN STEP, AND HE WILL
PLANT YOUR FEET ON HIGHER GROUND.

15

Live It!

He was a warrior of towering reputation. His enemies feared him greatly. More than anything else, they feared his sword, whose power had inspired wild rumors and legends. After hearing enough of these wild tales, his king finally demanded an examination of the notorious battle weapon. The warrior delivered his celebrated sword to the palace by special messenger.

The king examined the weapon closely before finally sending back this message: "I see nothing wonderful in the sword. I cannot understand why any man should be afraid of it."

The warrior must have smiled as he read the king's words, for he replied, "Your Majesty has been pleased to examine the sword, but I did not send the arm that wielded it. If you had examined that, you would have understood the mystery."

None of us, in our own strength, is any more impressive than that sword. But as we submit to the Holy Spirit and allow Him to wield us in the power of God, we become amazing instruments for God's glory. We can do all things through

Christ who strengthens us. The Spirit is God's powerful presence within us, and He makes all the difference in life.

THE SPIRIT IS ALIVE AND WELL

Next to our Lord's crucifixion and resurrection, I believe the arrival of the Holy Spirit at Pentecost was the most earth-shaking event in human history. As the Spirit arrived to transform the followers of Jesus, they in turn became transformers. The cowardly became courageous, and the defeated became dynamic.

> *If you are a Christian, the Spirit of almighty God lives within you.*

Soon the news of the gospel was spreading to every city, every nation, every cultural barrier. The Roman Empire itself was unable to withstand the Spirit's mighty momentum.

And I can assure you that the Holy Spirit is alive and well today. He desires to dramatically empower you. It remains only for us to follow His lead. If we do, we will surely duplicate or surpass the achievements of the first-century believers.

Paul admonishes us, "Since we live by the Spirit, let us keep in step with the Spirit" (Galatians 5:25 NIV). This verse paints a picture of moving forward with purpose, of walking with determination toward a goal. This is the picture I wish for you to fix in your mind as we finish this book. I pray that you will think of your future as a long and exciting track, leading you to higher ground with every step and finally to the finish line and a crown of life from the hand of the Master himself.

Remember, if you are a Christian, the Spirit of almighty God lives within you. He is always with you. And because of His empowering, indwelling, intimate presence, you can do anything that God desires for you. Walk in the Spirit, keep in step, and He will plant your feet on higher ground.

Readers' Guide

For Personal Reflection
or Group Discussion

Questions are an inevitable part of life. Proud parents ask their new baby, "Can you smile?" Later they ask, "Can you say 'Mama'?" "Can you walk to Daddy?" The early school years bring the inevitable, "What did you learn at school today?" Later school years introduce tougher questions, "If X equals 12 and Y equals –14, then …?" Adulthood adds a whole new set of questions. "Should I remain single or marry?" "How did things go at the office?" "Did you get a raise?" "Should we let Susie start dating?" "Which college is right for Kyle?" "How can we possibly afford to send our kids to college?"

This book raises questions, too. The following study guide is designed to: (1) maximize the subject material and (2) apply biblical truth to daily life. You won't be asked to solve any algebraic problems or recall dates associated with obscure events in history, so relax. Questions asking for objective information are based solely on the text. Most questions, however, prompt you to search inside your soul, examine the circumstances that surround your life, and decide how you can best use the truths communicated in the book.

Honest answers to real issues can strengthen your faith, draw you closer to the Lord, and lead you into fuller, richer, more joyful, and productive daily adventure. So confront each question head-on and expect the One who is the Answer for all of life's questions and needs to accomplish great things in your life.

Chapter 1: Longing for Intimacy

1. What forces might cause a person to feel helpless when confronting life?

2. What does it mean to call upon the Lord sincerely?

3. Which blessings bestowed on believers by the Holy Spirit do you cherish most? Why do you cherish those blessings so strongly?

4. Do you believe being filled with the Spirit is a mandate or an option? Defend your answer.

5. What area of life do you think Christians generally need to expose more fully to the Spirit's control? Why?

Chapter 2: Who Is the Holy Spirit?

1. How might a believer's relationship with the Holy Spirit change if he realized the Holy Spirit is a Person, not an "it"?

2. How do you know the Holy Spirit is God?

3. How would you describe the Holy Spirit's mission?

4. What main difference do you see in the Holy Spirit's relationship to Old Testament believers and believers today?

5. The author writes about the need to surrender to the Holy Spirit. What do you think this act involves?

CHAPTER 3: "YOU SHALL RECEIVE POWER ..."

1. Why do you agree or disagree that twenty-first-century believers can witness with as much power as Jesus' disciples did after Pentecost?

2. How would you contrast the disciples' lives before and after they received the Holy Spirit?

3. Do you believe Christians need more of the Holy Spirit? Why or why not?

4. What is the greatest challenge facing Christians today? How would the unlimited power of the Holy Spirit enable Christians to surmount this challenge?

5. Complete this statement: If the majority of Christians experienced the power of the Holy Spirit ...

CHAPTER 4: THE HOLY SPIRIT AND YOU

1. How can a Christian know the Holy Spirit lives in him or her?

2. When does the Spirit come to live in a believer?

3. What obstacles to being filled with the Spirit does the author cite?

4. How would you define "worldliness"?

5. What relationship, if any, do you see between being filled with the Scriptures and being filled with the Spirit? Defend your answer.

Chapter 5: How to Be Filled with the Spirit

1. What evidence of thirsting for more of Jesus do you see among Christians?

2. How does confession of sin enable the process of being filled with the Spirit?

3. Do you believe Christians need to repent? Why or why not?

4. What area(s) of your life do you need to surrender to the Holy Spirit? Will you do so?

5. Which is fully reliable: faith in God's Word or feelings? Defend your answer.

Chapter 6: Your Teacher of Truth

1. How does sin distort the truth?

2. If Pilate asked you, "What is truth?" how would you respond?

3. How does the Holy Spirit help us to see truth from God's perspective?

4. How has your regard for or understanding of the Bible changed since you became a believer? What credit for this change do you attribute to the ministry of the Holy Spirit?

5. Does the Holy Spirit place thoughts in our minds that cannot be confirmed by Scripture? Explain.

Chapter 7: Your Helper in Prayer

1. Why should believers pray privately? With other believers?

2. How is talking with God different from talking to God?

3. How does the Holy Spirit enrich our prayer lives?

4. What might happen when a believer asks God to remove a personal trial? What role might the Holy Spirit play in this scenario?

5. How can a believer cooperate with the Holy Spirit in His prayer ministry?

CHAPTER 8: YOUR MOTIVATOR TO HOLINESS

1. Why does the Holy Spirit want believers to lead holy lives?

2. What old habits has the Holy Spirit enabled you to cast off?

3. How do you explain the fact that Christians, who are new creations, still sin?

4. Why does a reverential fear of God act as a deterrent to sinning?

5. What insight from this chapter stands out the most to you? Why?

CHAPTER 9: YOUR COMFORTER IN ADVERSITY

1. What purpose do trials serve in the believer's life? How have trials made you better, not bitter?

2. How does the Holy Spirit help believers endure trials joyfully?

3. What impressed you most as you read the author's story about Corrie ten Boom?

4. Which is better: companionship with Jesus in the midst of adversity or living without Jesus in the midst of prosperity and ease? Defend your answer.

5. How can a believer confront trials optimistically?

CHAPTER 10: YOUR PEACEMAKER IN CONFLICT

1. How is it possible to enjoy personal peace in a strife-worn world?

2. On what basis does God grant individuals peace?

3. What bond exists among Christians because of the Holy Spirit's ministry? What issues does Satan use to try to disrupt this unity?

4. How does Spirit-given love manifest itself in a congregation of Spirit-filled believers?

5. How does humility enable us to see things from another believer's perspective?

CHAPTER 11: YOUR PROTECTOR FROM EVIL

1. Why are we foolish to try to win spiritual battles by using only our own resources?

2. How does each of the following enemies try to defeat Christians: the world, the flesh, and the Devil?

3. What sins of the flesh are seldom discussed in your circle of Christian friends? Are those sins insignificant? Why or why not?

4. What does it mean to crucify the flesh?

5. What insight from this chapter convicted or ministered to you as you thought about your struggles with sin? What step(s) will you take to apply what you've learned?

CHAPTER 12: YOUR SOURCE FOR SERVICE

1. What work does God perform in the life of every Christian? Specifically, what has He been doing recently in your life?

2. What special gifts can you commit to God?

3. Why does the Holy Spirit grant special gifts to believers?

4. Why is love essential to the effective employment of spiritual gifts?

5. How will you use your spiritual gift(s) to edify fellow believers this week?

CHAPTER 13: YOUR EMPOWERMENT FOR EVANGELISM

1. What fears might keep a Christian from sharing the gospel?

2. How does "bearing witness" differ from "witnessing"?

3. What Scripture references do you think are most beneficial in sharing God's plan of salvation?

4. What is the difference between arguing and showing concern when you share the gospel?

5. The author emphasizes the importance of these words in the soul-winning process: speak, stay, and seek. In your own words, summarize the underlying guideline for each word.

CHAPTER 14: YOUR COUNSELOR IN DECISION MAKING
1. Why do you agree or disagree that God has a specific plan for every believer?

2. How does knowing that Jesus is your Shepherd encourage you?

3. How does the Spirit reveal God's will?

4. What conditions, if any, does a believer need to meet in order to discover God's plan for his or her life?

5. How can godly believers help you discern God's will?

CHAPTER 15: LIVE IT!
1. How long does the Holy Spirit stay with a Christian?

2. Do you see the Christian race as a sprint or a marathon? Defend your answer.

3. What does the author identify as the second most earth-shaking event in human history? Why do you agree or disagree with him?

4. In the context of Philippians 4:13, what does it mean to be able to do all things through Christ?

5. What decisions will you make as a result of studying about the ministry of the Holy Spirit?

Appendix A

Satisfied?

SATISFACTION: (N.) FULFILLMENT OF ONE'S NEEDS, LONGINGS, OR DESIRES

The following is a brief presentation we have found effective in helping Christians understand the ministry of the Holy Spirit in their lives.

What words would you use to describe your current experience as a Christian?

Growing	Frustrated	Vital
Disappointing	Fulfilled	Guilty
Forgiven	Stuck	Empty
Struggling	Joyful	Mediocre
Defeated	Exciting	Dynamic
Up and down	Painful	Intimate
Discouraged	Duty	So-so
Others?		

Do you desire more? Jesus said, "If anyone is thirsty, let him come to me and drink. Whoever believes in me, as the

Scripture has said, streams of living water will flow from within him" (John 7:37–38 NIV).

What did Jesus mean? John, the biblical author, went on to explain, "By this he meant the Spirit, whom those who believed in him were later to receive. Up to that time the Spirit had not been given, since Jesus had not yet been glorified" (John 7:39 NIV).

Jesus promised that God's Holy Spirit would satisfy the thirst, or deepest longings, of all who believe in Jesus Christ. However, many Christians do not understand the Holy Spirit or how to experience Him in their daily lives.

The following principles will help you understand and enjoy God's Spirit.

THE DIVINE GIFT

DIVINE: (ADJ.) GIVEN BY GOD

God has given us His Spirit so that we can experience intimacy with Him and enjoy all He has for us.

The Holy Spirit is the source of our deepest satisfaction.

THE HOLY SPIRIT IS GOD'S PERMANENT PRESENCE WITH US.

Jesus said, "I will ask the Father, and he will give you another Counselor to be with you forever—the Spirit of truth."

JOHN 14:16–17 NIV

THE HOLY SPIRIT ENABLES US TO UNDERSTAND AND EXPERIENCE ALL GOD HAS GIVEN US.

"We have not received the spirit of the world but the Spirit who is from God, that we may understand what God has freely given us."

1 CORINTHIANS 2:12 NIV

The Holy Spirit enables us to experience many things:

- A genuine new spiritual life (John 3:1–8)
- The assurance of being a child of God (Romans 8:15–16)
- The infinite love of God (Romans 5:5; Ephesians 3:18–19)

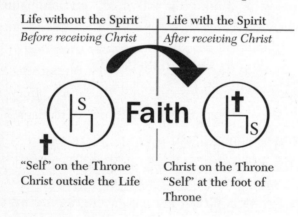

Life without the Spirit	Life with the Spirit
Before receiving Christ	*After receiving Christ*

Faith

"Self" on the Throne
Christ outside the Life

Christ on the Throne
"Self" at the foot of Throne

"The man without the Spirit does not accept the things that come from the Spirit of God, for they are foolishness to him, and he cannot understand them, because they are spiritually discerned."

1 CORINTHIANS 2:14 NIV

"The spiritual man makes judgments about all things ... We have the mind of Christ."

1 CORINTHIANS 2:15–16 NIV

"But those who are controlled by the Holy Spirit think about things that please the Spirit."

ROMANS 8:5

Why are many Christians not satisfied in their experience with God?

THE PRESENT DANGER

DANGER: (N.) A THING THAT MAY CAUSE INJURY, LOSS, OR PAIN

We cannot experience intimacy with God and enjoy all He has for us if we fail to depend on His Spirit.

People who trust in their own efforts and strength to live the Christian life will experience failure and frustration, as will those who live to please themselves rather than God.

We cannot live the Christian life in our own strength. "Are you so foolish? After beginning with the Spirit, are you now trying to attain your goal by human effort?" (Galatians 3:3 NIV).

We cannot enjoy all God desires for us if we live by our self-centered desires. "For the sinful nature desires what is contrary to the Spirit, and the Spirit what is contrary to the sinful nature. They are in conflict with each other, so that you do not do what you want" (Galatians 5:17 NIV).

THREE KINDS OF LIFESTYLES

A Self-centered Life	A Christ-centered Life	A Self-centered Life
Before receiving Christ	*After receiving Christ*	

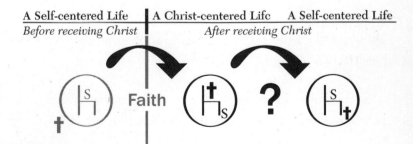

"Brothers, I could not address you as spiritual, but as worldly—mere infants in Christ. I gave you milk, not solid food, for you were not yet ready for it. Indeed, you are still not ready. You are still worldly. For since there is jealousy and quarreling among you, are you not worldly? Are you not acting like mere men?"

1 CORINTHIANS 3:1–3 NIV

How can we develop a lifestyle of depending on the Spirit?

THE INTIMATE JOURNEY

JOURNEY: (N.) ANY COURSE FROM ONE EXPERIENCE TO ANOTHER

By walking in the Spirit we increasingly experience intimacy with God and enjoy all He has for us.

Walking in the Spirit moment by moment is a lifestyle. It is learning to depend upon the Holy Spirit for His abundant resources as a way of life.

As we walk in the Spirit, we have the ability to live a life pleasing to God.

"So I say, live by the Spirit, and you will not gratify the desires of the sinful nature ... Since we live by the Spirit, let us keep in step with the Spirit."

GALATIANS 5:16, 25 NIV

As we walk in the Spirit, we experience intimacy with God and all He has for us.

"But the fruit of the Spirit is love, joy, peace, patience, kindness, goodness, faithfulness, gentleness and self-control."

GALATIANS 5:22–23 NIV

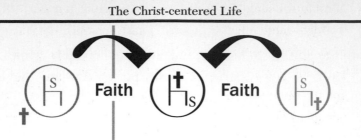

Faith (trust in God and His promises) is the only way a Christian can live by the Spirit.

"Spiritual Breathing" is a powerful word picture that can help you experience moment-by-moment dependence upon the Spirit.

Exhale: Confess your sin the moment you become aware of it—agree with God concerning it and thank Him for His forgiveness, according to 1 John 1:9 and Hebrews 10:1–25. Confession requires repentance—a change in attitude and action.

Inhale: Surrender control of your life to Christ, and rely upon the Holy Spirit to fill you with His presence and power by faith, according to His command (Ephesians 5:18) and promise (1 John 5:14–15).

How does the Holy Spirit fill us with His power?

THE EMPOWERING PRESENCE

EMPOWER: (V.) TO GIVE ABILITY TO

We are filled with the Spirit by faith, enabling us to experience intimacy with God and enjoy all He has for us.

The essence of the Christian life is what God does in and

through us, not what we do for God. Christ's life is reproduced in the believer by the power of the Holy Spirit. To be filled with the Spirit is to be directed and empowered by Him.

By faith, we experience God's power through the Holy Spirit.

> "I pray that out of his glorious riches he may strengthen you with power through his Spirit in your inner being, so that Christ may dwell in your hearts through faith."
>
> EPHESIANS 3:16–17 NIV

Three important questions to ask yourself:

1. Am I ready now to surrender control of my life to our Lord Jesus Christ (Romans 12:1–2)?
2. Am I ready now to confess my sins (1 John 1:9)? Sin grieves God's Spirit (Ephesians 4:30). But God in His love has forgiven all of your sins—past, present, and future—because Christ has died for you.
3. Do I sincerely desire to be directed and empowered by the Holy Spirit (John 7:37–39)?

By faith claim the fullness of the Spirit according to His command and promise:

God COMMANDS us to be filled with the Spirit.

> "… be filled with the Spirit."
>
> EPHESIANS 5:18 NIV

God PROMISES He will always answer when we pray according to His will.

"This is the confidence we have in approaching God: that if we ask anything according to his will, he hears us. And if we know that he hears us—whatever we ask—we know that we have what we asked of him."

1 JOHN 5:14–15 NIV

How to pray to be filled with the Holy Spirit …

THE TURNING POINT

TURNING POINT: TIME WHEN A DECISIVE CHANGE OCCURS

We are filled with the Holy Spirit by faith alone.

Sincere prayer is one way of expressing our faith. The following is a suggested prayer:

*Dear Father, I need You. I acknowledge that I have sinned against You by directing my own life. I thank You that You have forgiven my sins through Christ's death on the cross for me. I now invite Christ to again take His place on the throne of my life. Fill me with the Holy Spirit as You **commanded** me to be filled, and as You **promised** in Your Word that You would do if I asked in faith. I pray this in the name of Jesus. I now thank You for filling me with the Holy Spirit and directing my life.*

Does this prayer express the desire of your heart? If so, you can pray right now and trust God to fill you with His Holy Spirit.

HOW TO KNOW THAT YOU ARE FILLED BY THE HOLY SPIRIT

- Did you ask God to fill you with the Holy Spirit?
- Do you know that you are now filled with the Holy Spirit?

- On what authority? (On the trustworthiness of God himself and His Word: Hebrews 11:6; Romans 14:22–23.)

As you continue to depend on God's Spirit moment by moment, you will experience and enjoy intimacy with God and all He has for you—a truly rich and satisfying life.

An important reminder: Do not depend on feelings.

The promise of God's Word, the Bible—not our feelings—is our authority. The Christian lives by faith (trust) in the trustworthiness of God himself and His Word. Flying in an airplane can illustrate the relationship among fact (God and His Word), faith (our trust in God and His Word), and feeling (the result of our faith and obedience) (John 14:21).

To be transported by an airplane, we must place our faith in the trustworthiness of the aircraft and the pilot who flies it. Our feelings of confidence or fear do not affect the ability of the airplane to transport us, though they do affect how much we enjoy the trip. In the same way, we as Christians do not depend on feelings or emotions, but we place our faith (trust) in the trustworthiness of God and the promises of His Word.

NOW THAT YOU ARE FILLED WITH THE HOLY SPIRIT

Thank God that the Spirit will enable you:

- To glorify Christ with your life (John 16:14).

- To grow in your understanding of God and His Word
  (1 Corinthians 2:14–15).
- To live a life pleasing to God (Galatians 5:16–23).
  Remember the promise of Jesus:

> "But you will receive power when the Holy Spirit comes on
> you; and you will be my witnesses in Jerusalem, and in all
> Judea and Samaria, and to the ends of the earth."

ACTS 1:8 NIV

If you would like additional resources on the Holy Spirit,
please go to www.nlpdirect.com.

Adapted from *Have You Made the Wonderful Discovery of the Spirit-filled Life?* written by Bill Bright, © 1966.
Published by New Life Publications, P. O. Box 593684, Orlando, FL 32859

Appendix B

God's Word on Spirit-Filled Living

Following are selected Scripture references that were presented throughout the text of this book. We encourage you to sit down with your Bible and review these verses in their context, prayerfully reflecting upon what God's Word tells you about Spirit-filled living.

CHAPTER 1

John 14:12–14
Psalm 145:18

CHAPTER 2

Genesis 1:26
Genesis 3:22
Romans 1:4
John 14:16
John 14:12–13
John 10:10

CHAPTER 3

Acts 1:8

CHAPTER 4

Galatians 2:20
Romans 6
Romans 8:7
Mark 8:36
1 Corinthians 7:31
Matthew 16:26
Proverbs 29:25
Isaiah 59:2
James 4:8
1 John 1:9

CHAPTER 5

John 7:37–39

1 John 1:9
Romans 12:1–2

CHAPTER 6

John 16:13–14
2 Corinthians 10:5
Isaiah 55:8–9
1 John 2:27

CHAPTER 7

Philippians 2:13
Hebrews 10:19
Ephesians 2:18
Hebrews 4:16

Philippians 2:13
Romans 8:26–27
Hebrews 12:28
James 5:16
1 John 3:21–22
John 4:23

CHAPTER 8

1 Peter 1:16
Colossians 1:13–14
2 Corinthians 5:17
1 Corinthians 6:11
1 Corinthians 10:13
1 Thessalonians 5:23–24
Galatians 3:2–3
Galatians 5:16–17
Ephesians 6:10–12
Hebrews 12:29
Hebrews 10:31
2 Corinthians 7:1
2 Corinthians 5:21
Galatians 5:24
James 4:7
1 Corinthians 11:1
Philippians 4:8
Galatians 5:16

CHAPTER 9

James 1:2–4
Isaiah 43:2
Romans 8:38–39
John 16:33
Romans 8:28
1 Peter 5:7
2 Timothy 2:10
Psalm 50:15

2 Corinthians 4:16–18
Romans 5:3–4
1 Peter 4:19
1 Thessalonians 5:18

CHAPTER 10

Ephesians 2:14
Ephesians 4:4–6
1 Corinthians 8:6
Luke 11:4
1 Peter 4:8
Matthew 5:47
John 13:35

CHAPTER 11

Ephesians 6:12
Matthew 6:13
Ephesians 6:6–11
John 12:31
1 John 2:15–17
1 Peter 5:8
1 Corinthians 10:13
James 5:16
James 4:7–8
Ephesians 4:26–27
Psalm 34:7
Hebrews 4:12–13
Matthew 6:24
Romans 8:37

CHAPTER 12

Romans 12:4–5
1 Corinthians 13
2 Timothy 1:6
Romans 12:3
Galatians 5:13

Matthew 20:28
Romans 12:6–8

CHAPTER 13

Matthew 5:13
Matthew 5:14
Mark 16:15
2 Corinthians 5:20
Matthew 28:19–20
Luke 24:49
Isaiah 55:11
John 3:16
John 17:3
Romans 3:23
Romans 5:8
1 Corinthians 15:3–6
John 14:6
John 1:12
Ephesians 2:8–9
John 3:1–8
Revelation 3:20
1 John 5:11–12

CHAPTER 14

Jeremiah 29:11
Psalm 32:8
John 10:27
1 Thessalonians 5:17
Proverbs 16:9

CHAPTER 15

Galatians 5:25

About the Author

DR. BILL BRIGHT, fueled by his passion to share the love and claims of Jesus Christ with "every living person on earth," was the founder and president of Campus Crusade for Christ. The world's largest Christian ministry, Campus Crusade serves people in 191 countries through a staff of 26,000 full-time employees and more than 225,000 trained volunteers working in some sixty targeted ministries and projects that range from military ministry to inner-city ministry.

Bill Bright was so motivated by what is known as the Great Commission, Christ's command to carry the gospel throughout the world, that in 1956 he wrote a booklet titled *The Four Spiritual Laws*, which has been printed in 200 languages and distributed to more than 2.5 billion people. Other books Bright authored include *Discover the Book God Wrote, God: Discover His Character, Come Help Change Our World, The Holy Spirit: The Key to Supernatural Living, Life Without Equal, Witnessing Without Fear, Coming Revival, Journey Home,* and *Red Sky in the Morning.*

In 1979 Bright commissioned the *JESUS* film, a feature-length dramatization of the life of Christ. To date, the film has been viewed by more than 5.7 billion people in 191 countries and has become the most widely viewed and translated film in history.

Dr. Bright died in July 2003 before the final editing of this book. But he prayed that it would leave a legacy of his love for Jesus and the power of the Holy Spirit to change lives. He is survived by his wife, Vonette; their sons and daughters-in-law; and four grandchildren.